The McKenzies
of
Nesscroft

Rod McKenzie

Published by
McKenzie Family

December 2004

Nesscroft

Grandad McKenzie

Donald McKenzie was born in a village called Cabrich in Invernesshire, Scotland, in 1851. His parent's names were James and Margaret and he had four brothers and two sisters. His father probably provided for his family by working on an estate nearby. I have no knowledge of when Donald left Scotland or when he arrived in New Zealand, but it is presumed that he came to Port Chalmers as he was married in Dunedin in May 1874, when he was 23 years old. His bride was Maria Price Auld, who was born at Fort-William Scotland in the year 1857. She would have been a girl of 17 years when she married.

Maria Auld had migrated to New Zealand with her parents David and Isabella Auld, leaving Greenock on the Lady Egidia in January 1861. Maria had two brothers Jack and Dave and sisters Mary and Jemima, whom all lived in Dunedin.

I remember Dave and Mary well as they seemed to come quite often to "Nesscroft" to stay for a few days with Granny. The thing I remember about Dave was his jovial nature and the big piece of greenstone that hung from a gold watch chain stretching from pocket to pocket across the front of his waistcoat. He and my Dad (Rod) seemed to enjoy having fun together and he was always welcome at "Nesscroft". To me as a boy, Uncle Dave always looked well dressed and prosperous and it appeared to me that Granny resented a little his easy city life compared with her comfortless life.

Little is known about Donald and Maria between 1874 when they were married and 1878 when Donald's name appears amongst the names of shearers on Cannington Station. It is thought that they worked for some time on a farm in the Oamaru district during the years 1874-1878 and I believe this was quite likely.

Daniel or Donald

On the station receipts of shearers for 1878, his name is listed as Daniel McKenzie. Why he used the name Daniel is not known, but this was definitely the same person.

I inquired for information from Lena Munro, Dad's cousin in Scotland regarding his name and she confirmed that his name was Donald. The first time I heard the name Daniel was when I was about 12 years old. A neighbour who would have known Donald said to me "It's a wonder you weren't named Daniel after your Grandfather". I didn't understand what he was talking about as I always thought my second name Donald came from my Grandfather. I'm not even sure that Grandad could write and maybe the change came for that reason. His name on the shearing tally board at Cannington Station was always Dan McKenzie.

According to Cannington Station records Donald was one of the shearers in the 1878 shearing. There was also a Mrs McKenzie listed amongst the station employees that year and that would have quite likely been Maria. Donald continued to work on Cannington Station for a number of years.

In 1885, shearers were paid 16/6 per hundred ($1.65) and rousies about 2/6 per day (25c). The Cannington tally book for 1900 records that he shore 937 sheep in 13 days. On one day he shore 87 ewes. He also shore at Holme station and Craigmore woolsheds. The poplar trees that grew by the gate entering "Nesscroft" grew from sticks he carried home on his back as he walked home from shearing at Holme Station.

Long Walk
Grandad came to Cave by train with all his belongings, his dogs and a wheelbarrow. The railway had been extended from Washdyke through Cave to Albury in 1876. He loaded his possessions on the barrow, put his swag on his back and hitched his two dogs to the front. He then pushed the barrow up over the Cave hill and along the valley towards Cannington about 6 miles away. The shingle road was rough and often was not much more than a track. At the Pareora River, he had to unload the wheelbarrow and make several trips across to carry everything over. When he reached Nesscroft, he erected a shelter for the night.

Nesscroft
Daniel McKenzie bought 15 acres of land and built a house in November 1878 and named it "Nesscroft". It was very difficult to purchase a small area of land in those early years as the bulk of the land was held in large station holdings, which ran right from the sea to the mountains. In 1870 most of the large stations were still leasehold, but were under threat by farm freeholders buying up parts of the run.

Any person who wanted to freehold land could register his application at a land office in Timaru or Christchurch. The time would be recorded and the claim marked on a map. After payment had been made and the application approved by the Waste Land Board, a certificate would be issued to the owner. To prevent this from happening, the leaseholders would buy up small strips and access to water (gridiron).

The boundary between Cannington and Holme Station was fenced on the Holme station side of the White Rock River to avoid the several small streams flowing from the Cannington Station into the river. In 1874 Edward Elworthy, the runholder of Holme station, freeholded several strips running down to the boundary fence beside the White Rock River and the owner of Cannington had freeholded land around the homestead. This left the land between the road and the river free for Donald to purchase.

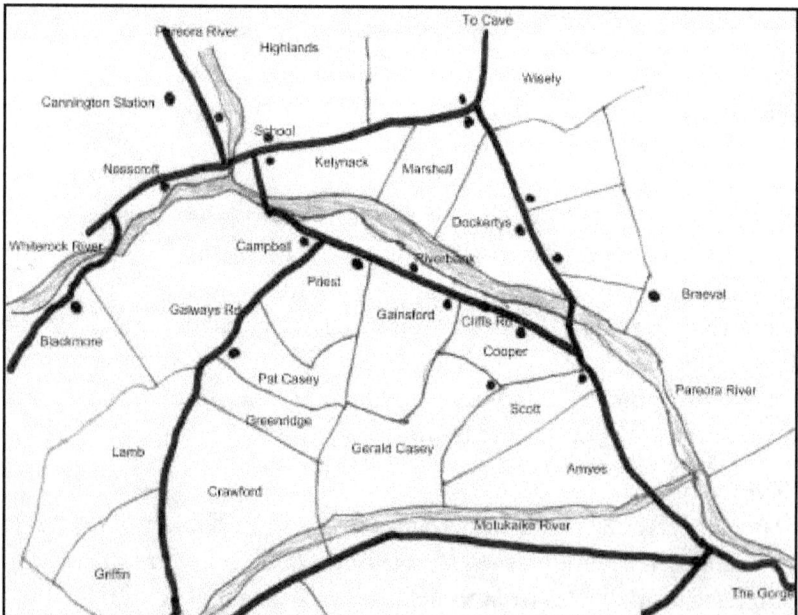

The piece of land that Grandad bought was a narrow strip of land. It was part of Cannington Station, but separated from the station by the road to Mt Nimrod making it of very little value to the station owner. The purchase price was about £2 ($4) an acre. As a shearer was earning less than £1 a hundred sheep shorn, and shearing an average of about 80 a day, money was also hard to come by.

The Nesscroft house was built of pit-sawn local bush timber and contained four main rooms and a lean-to scullery. Grandad had a chaff shed, six-horse stables and a two-horse loosebox built to accommodate a team of horses for contract work and two hacks for road travel. A good harness horse was essential for travel to Timaru by gig to do business and to bring home necessary supplies.

My memory of Grandad is very vague, as he died in August 1922, when I was five years old. I remember him as a man with a big beard, riding a chestnut horse, and with a black and white sheepdog called Scott.

Over the next seventeen years, he kept buying a few more acres until the total acreage in 1915 was about 50 acres.

> Twenty-seven years after the shearer Daniel McKenzie had freeholded his fifteen-acre farmlet on the banks of the White Rock River in 1878, he finally owned all of the river-side land between the bottom bridge on the White Rock River and its junction with the Pareora River.

> The section immediately above McKenzie's and another section were both freeholded by William Gill in 1878, and sold about two years later to a man named Warne, who farmed the sixty-one acre farmlet until early in 1887 when J.M. Ritchie bought it. Downstream from McKenzie's section the remaining riverbed leasehold was held by Ritchie until the expiry of leases in 1890.

> Upon the expiry of Ritchie's lease in 1890, the lower riverbed was let to McKenzie who also took over the small area across the river, originally Elworthy's, but abandoned by him when he had a fence erected on the terrace a few chains from the river, where it was safely above flood level.

> Finally in 1915 WT Ritchie, who owned the homestead block of Cannington after his father's death, sold the freehold paddock to McKenzie, giving him ownership of all the land (about 100 acres) between the road and the river, below the bottom bridge over the White Rock River (Noel Crawford - The Station Years).

In 1893 Grandad applied for forty more acres between the Cannington Road and the Pareora River. The ballot was won by Eli Rowe, who later obtained the block over the river, as part of the Rosewill Settlement, (it became part of Highlands).

Granny

I remember Granny well even though she would be quite elderly by that time. She was a very sprightly lady not very tall (about 5 ft) not overweight; her hair was brown with very few grey hairs.

Granny always spoke her mind. She was a very independent, capable lady, with a mind of her own and she would quickly put you in your place if she felt you were wrong. In spite of her abrupt way of speech, she was kind-hearted and as a child, I loved going with Dad to visit her. I loved the old house with the low ceiling in the lean-to part, the tall pine trees growing around the section, the large orchard and garden, with a spring of water in the corner to supply water for the garden. Dad would go up and see her each Sunday and I would often go with him. I seem to remember that she always had a mince or apple pie or both for dinner and I always enjoyed those visits.

Thinking back about Granny's life, I realise she was quite a remarkable woman. She was only 20 years old when she came to Cannington, to a small piece of land, with no house and no trees for shelter from the howling nor-west winds. Until the house was built, she and Donald must have lived in quite primitive conditions.

The nearest water was the White Rock River, three or four hundred yards down the terrace from the site of the house. Even when the house was built, it had no water laid on; just a 400-gallon tank at the corner of the house, so all the water was carried into the house. There was no sink in the bench, just a basin to wash the dirty dishes in. In those early days, Donald would be away shearing, sometimes fifteen miles away. The only means of travel would be to walk, so he would be away for a long day.

It must have been very lonely at times for a girl, with no close neighbours and no regular news or contact with the outside world. The nearest town was Timaru, 23 miles away. But in spite of the harshness of pioneer life, and the loneliness of being a young woman a hundred miles away from her family, I never heard her complain about the way life had treated her. She was a widow for twenty years.

The only bathroom she had was the river, where she bathed regularly. She managed for herself and milked three cows up to a few weeks before her death at 84 years.

Each year, she went to Dunedin for two weeks holiday with her sister. In 1941 when she went to Dunedin, she became sick with flu and this brought about her death.

Family

Maria and Donald had four children Belle, Alexander, James (Jim) and Roderick (born 1885). Belle left home quite young and went to Christchurch and got a job as a housekeeper. She hated the country and once left a position in Christchurch because she heard a rooster crow and thought it was too close to the country. I think Granny thought she should stay at home. She used to come down quite often, but she never got on with her mother and that made it quite awkward. She thought that everyone should be living like people in town. Belle did not marry and lived all her life in Christchurch.

Alex married Cecelia. They had one daughter Maisie, who died when she was 21 years old.

James (Jim) married Mary. They had two girls Agnes and Rita and two boys Donald (Donny), and Roderick (Roddy). He was living in Waipahi and working on the railway when I first got to know him. I presume that he started working on the railway at Cave and then transferred. He always came each year to visit Granny. He was very good-natured.

Information from Otago Early Settlers Museum

Maria Price Auld was the daughter of David and Isabella Auld. On 12 October 1860, they emigrated on board the "Lady Egidia" leaving from Greenock, Renfrewshire, Scotland. They arrived at Port Chalmers in Otago on 28 January 1861. Maria Price Auld was three years old. Her younger brother died at sea and her young sister Mary was born at sea.

David Auld had been born at Rothesay, Buteshire, Scotland. He married Isabella Girdwood on 19 June 1856 at North Bute, Argyllshire, Scotland.

In May 1863, David Auld was listed as a dairyman living in Anderson's Bay. When he died in 1919, he was living in Somerville Street, Andersons Bay, Dunedin. He was buried in Andersons Bay cemetery.

Isabella Girdwood Auld was born in 1830. She died on 21 November 1925.

David and Isabella Auld had 6 children.

Maria Price, born 17 April 1857
James, born 25 Dec 1858, died at sea on 1 January 1861
Mary Girdwood, born at sea 11 Dec 1860, died 10 July 1950.
Isabella, born April 1863
Thomas, born 1865 died July 1918
David, born 1870, died 14 Dec 1939

Donald McKenzie was born in 1851 in Invernesshire. He was the son of James and Margaret McKenzie and the brother of Simon, Roderick, John, Catherine, Alexander, and Ann.

A young man called Donald McKenzie was a passenger on a ship called Wild Deer. Launched at Connell's shipyard in December of 1863, Wild Deer began life as a China tea clipper. In this capacity, she made some very speedy voyages, but was applied to the New Zealand run in 1871 and made 10 successful voyages to New Zealand as a comfortable immigrant ship. Donald McKenzie was on the Wild Deer's first voyage to Dunedin. He departed from Greenock on 22 March 1871. He arrived in Port Chalmers on 21 June. He gave his departing address as 43 Warnock Street, Glasgow.

Travelling on the same vessel was a domestic servant named Ann Auld. Her address was Baldridge House, Dunfermline. She was born in born in 1845, so she was five years older than Donald.

Presumably, she was related to David and Isabella Auld, and might even have stayed with them when she arrived in Dunedin. If Donald McKenzie visited the family, this would explain how he met Maria Auld.

Donald McKenzie and Maria Price Auld were married in Knox Church Dunedin on 19 May 1874, three years after he arrived in the new settlement. The church marriage register records his name as Daniel McKenzie. He is listed as "full age". Maria is recorded as 17 years. They bought Nesscroft 1882

Donald and Maria had four children
Alexander
Belle
James (Jim)
Roderick

This clock belonged to Maria McKenzie.

Roderick and Maggie

Roderick

Roderick, my dad, married Margaret Wisely in May 1915, at Balfour Farm, the home of her brother Robert, in Cannington. Margaret was the daughter of Alexander and Helen Wisely of Milton, Otago. Alex Wisely was born in 1840 at Drumblade, Aberdeenshire. He migrated to New Zealand on the Grasmere in September 1862.

Helen Wisely was the daughter of James and Margaret Adam. She arrived in Dunedin on the Philip Laing with her parents in 1848 as a two-year old. Alex and Helen were married at Bon Accord, near Milton in 1878. Alex worked as a ploughman until he was able to buy a farm.

Margaret (Maggie) was born on 21 March 1887. She had four brothers James, John, Alexander, and Robert, two sisters Bessie and Nellie. When John and Robert came north to Temuka to take up farming, came with them as their housekeeper.

When John married, Robert bought a farm in Cannington, Balfour Farm, later called Pine Terrace. Margaret continued to be his housekeeper and met Rod McKenzie whom she later married.

I am not sure what work Dad did in his youth, but I presume he worked on neighbouring farms. Later he had a team of horses and worked as a contractor on Cannington Station and neighbouring farms.

Dad always had good horses, and I can remember travelling to Timaru with Dad and Mum in the gig with "Gypsy Grey" in the shafts. Gypsy was a great harness horse and if you let her have her head on the journey home, she would fair fly along. From

Cannington School
1896

Cannington to Timaru, farmers would journey over the Pareora Gorge Hill and up the Fairview zigzag. I can remember getting out of the gig with Dad and walking up the hill to lighten the load for the horse. On arriving in town, the horse would be put in a stable where it would be rested and fed ready for the journey home. A good harness horse could travel up to ten miles an hour, depending on the weight of the load and the condition of the road.

A harness horse pulled on a breastplate across its shoulders that was attached to the axle of the gig by leather traces. The shafts were attached to the harness that went around the girth of the horse. The seat on the gig could be adjusted, so that the shafts were "light on" to the harness. If it was "heavy on", the gig would give a rough ride when the horse trotted. We also had an old buggy. Dad would use it at harvest time to take out food for the men, but we never used it to go out as a family.

Horseman

Dad used to breed and break in his own horses, as he was a good horseman. I remember seeing him break in a young horse with only a strong post out in the paddock. Some ropes that he had made himself were the only aids he had.

Not having a stockyard, the unbroken horse would be driven with several other horses down the road to Mr Coopers, where there was a bit of a yard at the front of the stable. Dad would run the horses into the yard and lasso the one he planned to break. He would pull it up to a strong post and put a halter on it. He would tie a long rope to the halter and then drive all the horses home, with one dragging the rope. He would put all the horses in the small horse paddock by the stable.

The horses were driven close to a strong post planted out in the paddock. When the unbroken horse was passing the post, trailing the rope behind him, Dad would quickly seize the end of the rope and wrap it around the post. The horse was caught and the fun would start. Later he built a stockyard to make this work easier. There were always foals being born in the spring and young, unbroken horses running out in the river-bed until they were three or four years old, at which age they were broken in to work.

Riverbank

Grandad bought 149 acres of land about two and a half miles further down the Pareora River and along with this was about 100 acres of riverbed lease. This was land that had been part of Holme Station, the Pareora River being the boundary between Holme Station and the Levels run. The boundary was fenced on the Levels side of the Pareora River. The Cliffs road had cut this piece of land off and it was of very little value to the owners of Holme Station, so had been sold.

The leased land had been taken up by the Timaru Council to supply the growing town with water, it was rented out at a low rental and one of the terms of the lease was that the leasee had to keep the waterway free of dead animals.

When Dad and Mum married in March 1915, they took over that piece of land mentioned above and set up home about halfway between the Cliffs bridge and Martin's Crossing, which formed the boundaries at each end of the property.

Riverbank House

A house of four main rooms plus a scullery-pantry and washroom was planned and built. The two front rooms were a bedroom and a sitting room. At the back, there was a living room and a bedroom. A six-horse stable and shed for storing chaff for horse feed was built at the same time.

A small shed, which was called the "coal shed", was built adjacent to the house for the storage of coal, garden tools and odds and ends. A small corner of this building was enclosed and a door opened outside for a toilet. As children, we called this room the "W". I suppose this term coming from the word water closet (WC), but of course, there was no water. Under the seat in this little room was a four-gallon bucket which had to be emptied every week and the contents buried—a very unpleasant task.

This was a very humble and hard beginning for Rod and Maggie as they began their life

18

together. Life would be quite different for the housewife. Cooking was done on the coal and wood stove in the kitchen or living room, this supplying heat also for this room where the family spent time when inside.

A small water container on the end of the stove held about 2 gallons of water. A tap at the bottom allowed warm water to be taken out when needed, and cold water was poured in through the lid at the top to maintain the supply.

The only water laid on for all purposes was a tap in the sink in the scullery, the water coming from a four-hundred gallon tank catching rainwater off the roof. The bench and sink in the scullery were where all the baking and cleaning was done. Any hot water needed was provided by the stove and the big kettle always near boiling on top of the stove.

The pantry (storeroom) next door to the scullery was a small room with shelves around all walls. All foodstuffs were stored there, except meat, which was hung in a flyproof meat-safe placed in a shady site under a tree. In summer some meat would be pickled in a salt brine to make it last until the next sheep was killed. There was no bathroom in the house; all personal washing was done in a hand basin placed in the sink or a small tin bath set on the floor in front of the fire.

The washhouse, a room with a concrete floor, contained a big copper enclosed in bricks for boiling clothes, with wooden tubs alongside where boiled clothes were rubbed, rinsed, and wrung by hand. Monday was washing day and an early start was made to get the copper boiled and the clothes hung out to dry, making it a long, hard day for the housewife. Water was supplied from a four-hundred gallon tank catching water off the roof and even though there was a drain from the tubs, the dirty water was often carried out in buckets to water the garden. Water was always in short supply.

Other homes had been established on the road, later called Cliffs Road. The Gainsford family's home was a 1/4 of a mile east towards Timaru and Doxon Priest and family lived a 1/4 of a mile west, so the home was not nearly as isolated as Nesscroft.

In the early days, there were no trees around the house. The first trees Dad planted died because it was too dry. Later there was a Macrocarpa hedge around the southwest side of the house. A hedge of lilac went from the tank to the back gate, and a large laburnum grew beside the gate.

There was an orchard down the bank at the back of the house. A dry creek bed ran through it. The creek crossed the road up by Priest's house and a channel had been cut straight out to the river. It would have been dug out with a horse and scoop, before I can remember. When it overflowed in a flood, water would flow down the old creek bed behind the house. There was a pond in the old creek bed, but we never played near it, because it had been instilled in us that it was dangerous.

The cowshed at Riverbank was under the poplar and willow trees beside the orchard. It was built out of railway sleepers and corrugated iron.

Firewood

Firewood was scarce, so wood would have to be carted from the bush by horse and dray. In my young days, much of the firewood came from gorse sticks, taken from gorse out in the riverbed that had been through a fire. Much of it coated in sooty black bark making it very dirty to handle.

As willow trees that had been planted for flood protection grew big enough for branches to be cut off, these were also used for firewood. Those planted to protect the road opposite "Parira" were a ready source. This area, we called the "willows", was a place where we as children spent many happy hours playing and also working.

The biggest branches were cut down and towed home by a horse to be cut up for firewood by axe. No motorised saws in those days. We were trusted when quite young to take Gordie, a big draft horse, and spend Saturday dragging branches up the paddock home. Keeping up the supply of firewood was a constant chore, both getting it home and cutting it up small enough to go in the stove.

Coal was also used on the fire, especially at night to keep the fire alive until morning. This coal came from a mine at Chamberlain, Albury and would come to Cave loose in a railway truck and would be carried home by horses and dray. It would have to be shovelled to the dray and shovelled off into the coal shed. Looking back through one of Dads diaries, I could see that much time was spent carting wood and coal, for the "Riverbank" home and sometimes for Granny at "Nesscroft".

New Family
1916 was a happy year for Dad and Mum as on Feb 29 their first child Helen was born, beginning a family of five. I was born the

following year on 20 July. According to the birth notice, Dad was still in camp at Trentham. He returned home a week after I was born.

Dad told me that I was named after a Scottish hero called Roderick Mackenzie.

> Roderick Mackenzie was the son of an Edinburgh goldsmith who served as an officer in Bonnie Prince Charlie's army and had performed heroically in battle against the English. He struck up a friendly rapport with the Prince and they were known to enjoy each other's company. His appearance bore an uncanny resemblance to the prince himself.
>
> When the Prince suffered a terrible defeat at Culloden near Inverness in April 1746, a £30,000 reward was placed on his head, so thousands of English troops scoured the highland glens looking for him. One day they were both cornered by hostile troops about 10 km west of Inverness. Mackenzie appeared drawing the advancing troops away. He was cut down by a soldier's bullet and as the successful soldiers approached him, he cried out "You have murdered your prince". The jubilant soldiers carried his head back to Inverness. By the time they discovered their mistake, the real prince had escaped.

This explains why Roderick was a common name in our family. Mum always called dad Rod, so I was always called Roddy. When Dad died, Mum started calling me Rod.

War

War

These years were overshadowed by the World War that was being fought in Europe (1914-1918). Great Britain was involved, and this affected New Zealand, as it was part of the British Empire.

Many young men went overseas to take part in this war, which was to see many of them killed or wounded. There was great pressure placed on young men of military age to join up and go overseas to fight in this war that was to end all wars. One method used to make young men loyal and volunteer for service was to receive a letter through the post, in an envelope with a white feather in it.

I don't have any factual information as to when Dad joined the army to train for service overseas, but a family photo shows Helen as 1 year 10 months and myself as a baby of 5 months and Dad in army uniform. As I was born in 1917, this photo would have been taken in Dec 1917. It would appear that he was probably on final leave before going overseas, as the next information I have is a letter written to Mum from Salisbury, England, where there was a training camp for final training before being transferred to the battlefield in France. There isn't any date on this letter, but it is written during harvest time, which would be early 1918.

Another letter written on the 31 of November 1918 tells that he is in Dover on the way to France. I know that Dad was wounded by shrapnel in the hip not long after he began active service on the battlefield and later was returned to an English hospital to recover from the wound.

By this time, the war would be over and a postcard written on the 27th of January 1919 tells that he is released from hospital and is visiting uncles and Aunts in Glasgow and Inverness and would soon be on his way home.

One can imagine that this would be great news for Mum after having been separated from her husband for 18 months, living under the fear and dread of war, wondering if she would ever see her husband alive again.

It is hard for us today with the speed that news and mail travels to understand how slow letters would be in coming. A ship would take up to two months to sail from England to New Zealand and it would be months before Mum would know what was happening on the other side of the world. I remember Mum telling me that she didn't know that the war had ended until the Cabot boys called in on the way home from school with the news.

Military Record

Military training commenced (C Coy 29th Regiment)	28.5.17
Transferred to 34th NCOs Trentham, near Wellington to be trained as a corporal.	27.6.17
Promoted to Corporal (34th NCOs)	6.7.17
Allocated to Service Command	23.2.18
Embarked in Wellington on SS Tofua No 1 (The ship must have stopped at Colombo in Ceylon and Aden in Yemen on the way there, because postcards and photos were sent from these cities. The steamship would have stopped for bunkering coal.)	2.3.18
Disembarked in Suez and marched into the Australian Camp.	8.4.18
Admitted sick in Government Hospital in Egypt. His war record says he had bronchitis, but in a postcard to his parents, he said that he had pneumonia.	15.4.18
Discharged to duty	4.6.18
Embarked from Alexandria on the Ormond	4.7.18
Disembarked at Southampton	18.7.18
Entered Sling Camp, Wiltshire. (According to the postcards he sent home, he visited Stonehenge, Figheldean Village and Salisbury Cathedral. London was only 75 miles away, so he visited there when he was on leave. He brought a watch while in London.)	
Proceeded overseas to France via Southampton Arrived in Etaples (a port in northern France).	30.9.18
Joined 1st Battalion, Canterbury The Battalion was resting near Gouzeaucourt Posted to 13th Company as a private.	7.10.18

On 8.10.18, as part of the Battle of Cambrai, the 2nd and 3rd brigades crossed the canal and advanced to the village of Esnes. The 1st brigade which included the 1st Canterbury battalion remained in reserve. At 4 pm, the Canterbury battalion moved across the Escaut Canal ready to lead the attack on the next day. At midnight, the 1st Canterbury moved to its assembly positions; the attacking companies, the 2nd on the right and the 13th on the left, being on the Selvigny-Longsart road, north-west of Haucourt.

The advance began on October 9th at 5.30 am under a barrage. No opposition was encountered at first, and it soon became clear that the enemy had retired during the night. The barrage became rather a hindrance than a help, especially as there were many complaints of short shooting. They reached the Cambrai-Caudry railway at 9 am without opposition, and without casualties beyond those caused by their own shells.

Wounded in action with a gunshot injury to his thigh 9.10.18.
(Rod wrote that he was wounded by shrapnel, so it
is quite likely that he was hit by friendly fire.)

Admitted to a Casualty Clearing Station 9.10.18

Moved to a Base Hospital 11.10.18

Transferred back to UK 18.9.18

Admitted to Royal Victoria Hospital at Netley 20.10.18
(near Southampton).

Admitted to 1st NZ General Hospital, Brockenhurst in Hampshire for treatment of a shrapnel wound in the thigh	13.12.18
Admitted to 3rd General Hospital, Codford St Mary	7.1.19
Discharged to Command Depot	18.1.19
Admitted to 3rd General Hospital, Codford St Mary with bronchitis	19.2.19
Discharged from hospital	18.3.19
Visited relatives in Inverness and Glasgow	
Embarked from Glasgow on the Paparoa	1.4.19
Admitted to hospital on the Paparoa	7.4.19
Discharged from hospital	26.4.19
Disembarked in Wellington as a Lance Corporal	25.5.19
On Leave	26.5.19
Discharged as physically unfit for service	22.6.19
War Pension of 30/- per week approved for 6 months	28.7.19

Maggie

The year 1918 would have been a very difficult and lonely year for her, keeping a home going with two little children to care for and all the other chores that go with maintaining a farm home.

Grandad used to ride down from Nesscroft and look after the sheep and I guess he would do other jobs that a mother with two children could not do. Mum told me that when the cow calved, she couldn't get the calf to drink milk from a bucket. She told Grandad about this and he impatiently took the bucket of milk saying "trust a woman not to be able to feed a calf". He was soon back with the bucket empty and the calf unfed, as he had got annoyed with the calf's stubbornness, and tipped the milk over the top of the calf. He left it to Mum to battle with.

I guess there must have been many times when she would have wept at the harshness of life alone. She spent some of the winter at Nesscroft, but this wasn't a very happy time as she found caring for two children in Granny's home very difficult. There was a big snowfall that winter and snow lay on the Cannington flats for some weeks. Of course, I was too young to have any memory of that time and I don't remember either Mum or Dad ever talking very much about those years.

By reading between the lines of letters and using the dates that those letters were written, allowing for the pace of travel by ship in those days, one can assume that by the middle of 1919, Dad would be home on the farm at Riverbank and back into farming again. However, there would have been some changes during the time he was away.

Grandad & Helen

Family Life

Snow

A record snowfall occurred in 1917. Jim Little and Jim Stumbles, who were shepherds at Cannington rode their horses from the homestead up to the Pareora Gorge without seeing a fence. Their horses were able to walk over the fences on the frozen snow. They spent the whole winter skinning dead sheep as they emerged out of the snow.

Land Boom

With servicemen returning from war overseas and the government buying big blocks of land to cut up into farms for the settlement of the returning men, a land boom had taken place. The going rate for land was about £20 an acre and this was to prove to be far beyond its true value, as many of these new ventures failed financially. Wheat was in demand at that time. Some farmers did very well growing wheat during the war. For example, Mum's brother Alex had sold his farm and retired before he was 50 years old.

These early 1920 years were busy years on the farm, growing crop and harvesting the same. A man was employed some of the year, mainly to drive the team.

The harvest was done by working with neighbours. Everything brought to the farm or taken from the farm meant trips to Cave by horses and dray, a very slow means of transport when compared to today. A lot of days were taken up with this task until 1922 when a local man Hector Marshall bought a small truck (2 ton) and began to take over the transport of grain to the train at Cave.

Greenridge

My parents were caught up in this land boom in 1920 when they bought a 195-acre block from their neighbour Doxon Priest for £20 an acre. This block of land was up Galways Rd, nearly 2 miles from the Riverbank homestead. In Dad's diaries, this was called "Priest's Block" and in later years it was named "Greenridge". This land would be seen as suitable for the growing of wheat. Our strip went right across the back of Priest's farm. Pat Casey had purchased the strip in front of it. We could access it through the back of Mr Gainsford's farm or via Galways road.

When Dad bought Greenridge, it was only in two blocks and was poorly watered with two dams (ponds), so it needed a lot of development in the way of fencing and water supply. We fenced it into five paddocks using Cyclone netting. The back paddock was fenced into two paddocks. It had a dam for water, but this was really too small. The block at the front was fenced into three paddocks.

In the earlier years, we used to trek the team backward and forward between the two farms every day, but it was a terrible drag. Later, Dad took a hut up from Riverbank to Greenridge.

Dad had bought the hut from the County Council and used it for the man he employed during the summers to work the team. Most people in those days employed a man during the summer.

30

He put wheels on the back of the hut and a big pole on the front of it. The pole was fixed under the dray to the axle. He pulled the hut up the road with three horses in the dray. He had arranged with Pat Casey to be there with a couple of extra horses to help pull it up the hill. I was with Dad that day and I can still remember the excitement.

The wheels came off an old grubber belonging to the Campbell's, but it had sat in the ground for a couple of years and part of the wheels had rusted. Dad had strengthened them up with some timber, but when we got onto the road, it started to bump.

The bump got worse and worse, so Dad abandoned those wheels and took some off the binder and put them on. We had to jack the hut up to get the new wheels on. The move was all done in one day, but Dad had done a fair bit of work beforehand to get ready. We put the hut down in the valley by the dam where there would be water for the horses.

Nobody ever stayed overnight in the hut, but the horses would remain each night, when we were working up there. We would go up early in the morning and cook breakfast, while the horses were feeding. We could also shelter in the hut, while the horses were feeding at night. It was a tremendous help to be able to leave the horses up there.

Growing Family

This same year 1920, was also the year when the next child was born. A boy named Alan Gerdwood came into the world on May 31. This little boy, who was born when the world was excited about peace forever grew up to be a gentle, peace-loving man who would lose his life in a world war 23 years later.

On September 17 1921, the second girl in the family was born and named Margaret Isobel. I notice in Dad's diary on Aug 5 just two words, "May came" and presume this was May Tooley coming as housekeeper. On Aug 9, Dad took Mum to town to wait for the baby to arrive nearly six weeks later and it wasn't until Sept 30 that Mum returned home. I think Mum was staying with a Mrs Oborn during that time away from the family. May stayed on until Oct 29.

31

In August of that same year, Grandad McKenzie died, making Granny very dependent on Dad and Mum. Grandad died suddenly on the veranda at Nesscroft sitting in his chair waiting for the grocer to bring the newspaper and the grocer found him dead.

Rod and Helen

On April 24 1923, a third baby boy was born into the family and was named Alister Wisely. He was apparently born at home with a doctor and Nurse Brown in attendance, and a nurse staying on for another two weeks. The rest of the family were taken up to Grannies at Nesscroft, while this event was taking place.

Now the family was complete 2 girls and 3 boys, the eldest Helen would be seven years old and would be going to school at the Cannington School. There is no mention in the diaries of school activities, except on Dec 21 1922, the school picnic is noted and I guess this would be because Helen was attending school.

Cars

I also notice in the diary on Oct 28, Dad wrote "took Maggie, Helen and Roddy to town, left babies with May". I remember quite clearly going to town in the gig so I think that this would be the time. I remember Mum and Helen were there and I remember getting out of the gig with Dad and walking up a hill to make it easier for the horse, and I remember Gypsy the horse being put in the livery stables for the day. This was probably one of the last trips to town by horse and gig as in April 1922, as Dad bought a second-hand Model T Ford car for £160. The diary also notes that the following week was Easter Monday and the family went to the Fairlie show, this being the first of many.

When Dad first bought the car, it would not go into the shed. He dug out the floor, so that it would fit under the roof.

A couple of years later, Dad traded it in on a new Model T Ford. Dad was quite early in getting a car, because there were not a lot around at that time. Mr Lamb was the first person who had a car. The Model T Ford was a good car. A problem was that it was gravity fed, so if you were going up a steep hill when the tank was low, the petrol could cut out. You would have to turn the car around and back up.

The worst place was going up over the Pareora gorge. We would sometimes have to back down and turn around and go up backwards. It must have been a tricky manoeuvre on a rough, narrow road. There was only one really steep bit. That was where the road went up from the Cannington side.

Music

There was very little music in the early days. The only opportunities to listen to music were at the dances at Cave. The band would have a piano, a fiddle and sometimes an accordion. At home, we lived with silence. Granny had a phonograph that played from cylinders, but most people had no facility for playing music.

Stan Hewin worked on various farms around the district. He was a bit simple, but was a hard worker. I think he was related to Mrs Pat Casey. (In those days all the misfits lived in the country). He had a portable gramophone and a lot of records. Each night he would bike to a different home and spend the evening playing his records. In return, he would be given supper.

He started coming to our place when I was about 8 years old and would turn up once a week or fortnight. Mum got cross with him, because he mumbled and she could not understand him, but we all enjoyed the music. Later on, he would hire an aeroplane on a Saturday, and get the pilot to swoop over various houses he was going to visit. The next week he would call around and ask if people had seen him.

Travel to School

I remember starting school in 1922, being picked up by Miss Amyes, the teacher, who travelled each day in a dogcart pulled by a black horse called Bonnie. A "dogcart" was a two-wheeled vehicle like a gig, with a seat facing forward and another facing backwards being very suitable for the transport of children. Miss Amyes lived with her parents on their farm by the lower Pareora Gorge, their home being just where the Motukaika River crossed the road. She later gave up the horse and cart and rode a motorbike to school.

By that time, Helen and I would be able to walk to school along with other pupils who were walking or riding ponies. Those that were riding ponies came from the Motukaika district, a journey of five or six miles. I don't remember it being any hardship walking to school, and there was often fun with several children on the road together.

When Alan started school in 1925, we were travelling to school by horse and gig. Dad bought an elderly black mare we called Darky, who was very quiet and reliable to pull the gig.

Darky was not frightened of anything, so she was an excellent horse for children to use. She had been used for pulling a buggy and tank

34

to transport water to a traction engine, so was well used to all sorts of noises.

We all learnt to ride on Darky, and when Alan wasn't going to school, Helen and I would ride her together, called (double banking). I didn't like that much because Helen being the eldest, always held the reins and I thought that this should be the man's job. I did get my turn when Helen was sick and, of course, when she finished school, I had full charge. Actually, the horse would trot to school and back on her own, so she did not need much driving.

I had many happy hours riding Darky - I loved to ride her down the riverbed to bring the milking cows home at night or to go and round up the team of working horses on a Sunday night. They were always turned out on the riverbed on days they weren't being worked. I always rode without a saddle and imagined myself as a cowboy riding the range herding cattle.

Alan & Alister

The riverbed as we called the land outside the fenced paddocks was about two miles long and a 1/4 of a mile wide and was unfenced except for the boundary fences. There were no broom or blackberry bushes in those days, only scattered gorse which was always kept burnt, so it was a great place for a boy on a horse. It was a great place to run young unbroken horses and young cattle on, as there was always feed, shade, and water. It also carried about 300 ewes and their lambs.

The river had a lot more water, as the Timaru supply had not been taken from it. There were swamps and small lagoons with a lot of water.

Now back to school days. Darky and the gig solved any problem of getting the family to school and when Margaret's and Alister's turn came to go to school, we all went in the gig. In winter we would get off and run behind to get warm, hanging onto the gig. Sometimes a couple of the Priest children would be hanging on as well, but they would not be allowed to get in and ride. When we got to school, we would unharness Darky on the side of the road and then take her round to the pony paddock. Many children rode horses to school, some walked, and a few rode bicycles.

The roads were rough, as shingle crushers had not arrived on the road building scene and any shingle put on the roads was carted straight from the riverbed in drays pulled by three horses. Any stones that were a little too big were broken on the road by workmen wielding a light long-handled hammer. They held the stone under the toe of their boot and giving it a sharp hit with the hammer to break it. These men wore "glasses" made of light cloth to protect their eyes from flying stone chips. Often the best road maker was the big traction engine towing a big mill and three huts behind. We would enjoy running along the road barefooted following the engine tracks.

School

I didn't enjoy school very much as I had made up my mind that I was going to be a farmer and I didn't see much connection between what I was learning at school and what a farmer would need to know. School was very different from what it is today. At Cannington, there were a few over 30 children on the roll. It never quite made the 35 students needed to get two teachers.

I remember very little about my first day at school. One thing that remains in my memory of that first day at school was that one of the big girls, Jean Williams picked me up and carried me around and then kissed me before she set me down. What a terrible way to treat a boy at that tender age. But I do remember being fascinated with all the horses that were used to transport children to school.

Most of the big boys did not want to be at school, and they gave the teachers a terrible time. Bernie Lang could keep the teacher occupied for no end of time. We all felt safe when the teacher was battling with Bernie. He would lose his temper and refuse to do anything while the teacher stood over him, threatening him with the strap. She would lose her temper too and refuse to move until he started to work. This could take a long time, and we all felt safe while the battle raged.

Riverbank

Looking back, I feel very sorry for our teachers. They were probably quite young (we thought they were old) and not long out of college, keen to do something for the nation by teaching rural children. What a disappointment we must have been to them. I am sure that some nights they must have gone home and wept. We were an unwilling, stubborn lot, deciding to hate a new teacher before we met her, so there was no way she could succeed with us.

The boys always called the girls tarts, so behind her back, the teacher was known as the "Old Tart". There was a rule in the school that if a boy met the teacher in the school grounds, he was expected to stop and salute. I never ever saluted the teacher, as I made sure that we never met.

I looked upon the teacher as a sort of enemy, who was out to spoil life for me. I know now that I was quite wrong and I could have gained a lot more from my school days if I had understood what it was all about.

School Games

There was no sport or sports equipment in the school, so we had to make our own fun playing games of rounders, prisoners base, and all across, mostly unsupervised as the teacher seldom came out of the schoolroom.

One game we played was 'Anthony'. The entire school would divide into two teams, one on each side of the school. A ball would be thrown over the school with a shout of 'Anthony'. If the other team caught the ball before it touched the ground, they could run quickly around to the opposing team and hit as many as possible with the ball, and they became part of that team. This went on until one team had all the children on their side. The noise of this almost drove the teacher mad, and sometimes she would forbid us from throwing the ball over the school.

There seemed to be a continuing feud between the big boys and the girls. The boys played at war. The big boys built up barricades of logs and branches and pelted cones and chips at the opposing fort. The little boys, of whom I was one, were ammunition carriers and we had to scout around and gather up cones and chips to keep soldiers supplied with ammunition. I suppose this was a carry-over from the Great War, which was not long past, leaving most boys with the idea that war was great fun.

The girls played houses in the pine trees, building houses with rows of pine needles; the older girls being fathers and mothers and the little girls their families. They would be sweeping floors, having babies and cooking meals. Every now and then, the boys would burst in and wreck them. Occasionally a peace treaty seemed to be made, and the boys and girls would play together.

In spite of the drawback of having to go to school, I did enjoy those years of my life. We were a happy family, and we had lots of fun as a family, playing games that we made up. We never had a lot of toys, but I don't ever remember feeling deprived. We were always well fed and well clothed, and our home seemed to have an atmosphere of security where I always felt secure.

I guess my main desire in the latter part of my school days was to pass the exams at the end of each term and especially at the end of the year. I needed to get my proficiency at the end of standard 6 to leave school and embark on my career of becoming a farmer. I always did reasonably well in exams, generally gaining second place in the class, with Stewart Lamb always taking first place. I remember once getting a special prize at the end of the year for diligence.

School Picnics

Doxon Priest was chairman of the school committee for many years and did a lot for the school. Each year he would organise a school picnic (end of year break-up) at the homestead of Cannington Station. I looked forward to those functions for weeks, and we trained for the races that would take place. Everybody in the district turned out for it. Our parents sat in the shade of a big weeping willow tree and talked while we children ran bare-footed on the big lawn. What a joy it was to run on nicely trimmed lawn as very few people had lawns in those days. Lawn mowers were quite unknown, and even in the school grounds, the grass in the summer was up to a young child's knees.

We ran the races with great enthusiasm, as there was money to be won: one shilling for first, sixpence for second and a penny for third. If I went home with 1/6 in my pocket, I felt quite rich, as you could buy an ice cream for 1 penny. Everyone received a prize in the form of a book and some a special prize as well.

Obedience

Our parents expected obedience, but I don't remember them as heavy-handed. The worst punishment I remember was being shut out in the wash-house, which I remember as very humiliating. It seems to me looking back, that somehow, they expected respect and received it.

Speaking for myself, I would never have willingly done anything that I knew would disappoint my parents. Of course, there were times when I did things behind their backs that I knew I shouldn't do, like taking matches and live bullets to school. The bullets were placed on a stone at the far end of the playground and hit with another stone causing them to explode. We knew it was wrong but didn't realise the danger involved. I guess this act was really to be seen as important in front of one's mates.

I remember once pretending I was feeling sick as for some reason I didn't want to go to school. Apparently, I wasn't a very good actor because my parents saw through it. They didn't growl at me or seek to punish me in any way. About 9.30 Dad just quietly said to me that he was going to the stock sale at Pleasant Point and he would drop me off at the school on the way. He took me into the school and explained to the teacher how I had been feeling unwell earlier but was now all right. The fact that I remember clearly that incident 70 years later, shows the impact it had on me and I never tried that trick again.

Jack Kleim

Fred Kleim was a German, who married a widow when he came to New Zealand. She had two daughters. He eventually had to give up his farm because he had an alcohol problem. He worked as teamster for Mr Gainsford and also did a bit of work for Dad. I think that Dad thought he was a bit lazy. Once when he was harrowing for Mr Gainsford, he set up a cart behind the harrows to ride on. That was not the done thing.

I was intrigued by him saying, "I will have to get my kapoks". So we hitched up the buggy and went down to Gainsford's and got his mattress and pillow.

Once during the school holidays his son Jack came to stay with him for a holiday. When he went home, his father gave him 10 shillings, which he kept. He was living down in Southland with an Uncle, who made him hoe swedes when he should have been at school. Once when he was sent out to work, he ran away. He used the 10 shillings to buy a train ticket to Cave. When he arrived in Cave, Mr Baker gave him a ride on his dray to Scott's corner. He walked up the road to Gainsford's and when his father came home from work, he found him sleeping in his bed.

Mrs Gainsford felt sorry for Jack and allowed him to stay on as a sort of boarder. He went to school at Cannington. We did a lot of things together and became good friends. When he left school, he worked around the district, mostly for the Campbell's. Unfortunately, he had the same thirst for alcohol as his father. I lost touch with him after he went overseas during the war.

Rats

On a wet day, Alan, Alister and I would go rat hunting. The boards around the bottom of the shed had rotted, so the rats were able to get in. They would make an awful mess of the chaff bags. We should shine a light between the bags and if we saw one, we would shoot it with the 0.22. Alister had a dog called Tip, who was a brilliant rat catcher. When one ran out, he would catch it and shake it violently until it was dead. He had learned that they could not bite while he was shaking them. The rats also nested in the pig sty. They were very clever. When we set rabbit traps, they would cover them with straw, so they could walk over them.

Good Years

While all this was taking place and we were receiving our primary education, changes were taking place on the farming scene. Of course, I was quite unaware of this at the time as our parents did not discuss business or private family matters in front of us, so those years 1925-1930, apart from school, were very carefree happy days.

The post-war boom in the prices of farm produce made the early years of that decade prosperous for farmers. A lot of building was taking place and farms were being improved, cars were being bought and homes were having rooms added to them to accommodate growing families.

Looking back through Dads diary I note that in 1921 a fat lamb was worth £1 ($2), a fat wether 25/6 ($2.56), ewes 18/-, draft horses £20. The returns for 1921: Sheep £318 8/6, wool £127 13/7, wheat £133 10/3. Total £590 ($1180).

Compared with today, this doesn't seem much, but expenses for that year were only £345 leaving £245 for family expenses (About $15,000 when adjusted to current dollars). This was sufficient for a family to have a reasonable standard of living with some funds left over to put into developing the land. It needs to be remembered that a big proportion of the food needed came off the land – meat, milk, vegetables, fruit, eggs, and the feed for the horses, which were the power to work the land, was grown on the farm. Even the replacement horses were bred by farmers.

So, the first two-thirds of that decade were fairly prosperous times for farmers with the prices for farm produce tending to rise. I quote again from the diary that in 1925 the price for a fat lamb was 37/6 ($3-76) and a ewe 27/6, very good prices considering that a man could be employed for 30/- plus keep per week. Stock numbers would be about 400 ewes, 5 cows, 8 horses, 3 or 4 young horses. Lambing 112%.

At this time Jim Kelynack was driving the team and doing odd jobs for Dad for part of each year, having begun in 1923 and continuing for four or five years. There seemed to be a ready supply of casual farm workers available in Timaru for harvest etc. A gentleman named Mr Thoreau had an employment agency in the Royal Arcade in Timaru and a request message to him would result in a man arriving by train to Cave the next day. This same gentleman was also the secretary of the Farmers Union and I remember going with Dad to a meeting held in his office.

A sign of the times was the building of a lean-to implement shed on the back of the stable. The roof on the stable was extended to give the horses more protection from southwest rain. The timber and roofing iron for this was railed to Cave and carted to the farm by dray.

From 1923 onward, grain and wool were transported from the farm to the railway by Hector Marshall in a two-ton truck, so I am not sure why this timber was transported by dray.

Extensions to the House

About this time (1925), the Riverbank house was extended by three rooms, a lounge, a single bedroom and bathroom. The front room was a large sitting room and the bathroom was at the back. A veranda was built across the front of the house, which was a great place for us to play on wet days. Also, a hot-water cylinder was placed beside the coal stove to supply hot water to the bathroom and the sink in the scullery (kitchenette).

The work was done by a building contractor from Cave, Mr Douglas Cameron who travelled over each day on a motorcycle and sidecar. I think he would be a self-taught carpenter, but he did employ some other tradesmen at times. He could do everything himself, if necessary, (painting, paper-hanging plumbing, etc.) He was very slow and liked to talk a lot and Mum used to get frustrated with him as he would follow her around to finish telling her some story he had begun. She had to try and keep out of his sight, so that he got on with his work. Nevertheless, he was a good friend to our family and did many a job and good turn for us. He and his wife lived on a sixty-acre farm at Cave. They only had one child a boy (Murray) and they used to invite me over to play with him and I can remember having good times over there.

Pantry | Scullery | Wash

Parents | Living Room | Bathroom

Spare

Girls | Boys

Lounge

Veranda

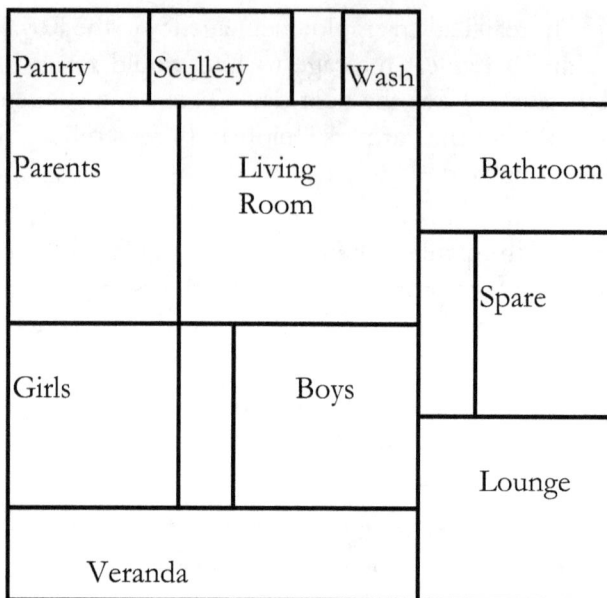

The extension to the house was a great blessing to us as a family as the girls had the west front bedroom and the boys the front room that had been the old sitting room. I slept on a stretcher in the corner (wire spring with folding legs) and Alister and Alan shared a double bed. We continued together in this room until I left home. Mum and Dad used the bedroom at the back beside the living room. The new single bedroom was a guestroom.

Telephone

It must have been about that time that telephone lines were erected around the district and everyone had contact with their neighbours and the rest of the country. The exchange was at Cave, and the district was divided into party lines where six to ten homes would form a group who could phone each other, but of course, they had to take turns in doing this. Each home had its own number and one would know when they were wanted when they heard their own ring, ours was two short rings and one long one. When you finished using the phone you gave a short ring to let your neighbours know that you were finished. If you wanted to ring outside your party line, you gave a long ring and the exchange would answer and connect you up with the number you wanted.

Deaths

In 1925 there were two deaths in Mums family. On July 25 her Father died at his home at Milton, and her brother Jim died from a tumour on his brain on Sept 22, also in the Milton district. On both of these occasions, Dad and Uncle Bob made the trip to Milton by car to attend the funerals.

This would be quite a long journey in those days. Mum stayed at home with the family as I suppose was the custom. I only remember Mum once going south to Milton, where she was brought up. She once went to Waipara a little north of Christchurch, so she travelled very little in her lifetime.

Electricity

Another highlight in those years (about 1928) was the coming of electricity to the Cannington district. The line came over the hill from Cave and around the block where our farm was. Cliffs Rd was quite early getting electricity, as there were a lot of people in one place, making it easier to put it in. Each recipient had to agree to a guarantee for five years; ours was £5 a year. This seems very little today, but I remember that my parents thought it was quite expensive. Contractors came and put lights in every room plus one outside in the porch, a stove in the scullery and several points for three-point plugs. The amount of power they used didn't amount to anywhere near the £5 guarantee they were paying.

The electric power was a great boon. No more women standing over a hot coal range and chopping wood to feed it; no more reading in a poor light in the living room. One of the worst features of the kerosene lamp was that you went into darkness as soon as you went out of the room with the lamp. Candles were not encouraged for children because of the danger. We just had one good lamp in the living room. To have a light in each room was a real luxury.

Of course, the coal stove in the living room was kept burning, especially in the winter, as this was the source of hot water and heating for the living room. I think Mum still did quite a bit of cooking on the coal range, as a lot of the year it was burning anyway. However, the amount of wood needed was reduced a lot. The porridge for breakfast was always made on that stove and the big black kettle was always quietly singing away, almost boiling.

It was my job to cut what was called "the morning wood", that was a petrol tin filled with wood cut fairly small and topped up with kindling and placed in the porch each night ready to light the morning fire. I loved this task of cutting wood and if someone, trying to be helpful did it for me, I would feel quite offended.

Riverbank with Extension

Another job I liked was filling two buckets with coal ready for the following day. In the winter, I would try and leave it until it was getting dark and then I would be able to take a candle into the dark coal shed. There I would break up the big lumps of coal with a big hammer and shovel it into the buckets, imagining that I was a coal miner working down in a mine. I think I had a pretty lively imagination when I was a boy. I could change easily from being a cowboy riding the range to a coal miner working a mine.

Falling Prices

While all these good things were happening to us as children at school and at playtimes at home, things were not going so well on the farming scene. Prices of farm produce were starting to come down and by 1928-29 farmers were starting to feel the pinch. Land prices were coming down and interest rates were seen to be high. Some farmers had two and three mortgages and were paying up to 8% interest.

Many farmers had over-borrowed and were finding it impossible to keep up their interest payments. Fortunately, our parents had not done this, so they were not embarrassed in this way, but with the changing lifestyle brought about by modern technology and a growing family, the cost of living was gradually going up. Being of a thrifty nature, they were always careful to live within last year's income.

Proficiency

I loved to read. I read all the books in the school library several times. I also got books from the library at Cave. The store cart would bring them out for me. They were mostly adventure books. I would re-tell the stories to Alan and Alister when we had gone to bed at night. I was always happy if I had a book to read.

1930 was an exciting year for me as it was to be my last year at school, provided I qualified for my proficiency certificate at the end of the year. I worked hard at school, as I don't think I would have been allowed to leave school without it. It was quite an ordeal for a shy country boy to go over to the Cave school where we had to sit the exam, but it was a thrill when word came that I had passed. I guess I thought I was quite well qualified at that time.

Tommy

I could ride my own horse well. Dad had broken in Gypsy's grey foal for me when he was four years old and rode him until he was quiet enough for me to ride. A couple of years earlier, I had seen Dad break him in and he was a fiery little horse that didn't give in easily.

Once Dad had put a halter on him, he began the process of teaching him to lead, tie up, to be saddled and allow all his legs to be handled. Then came the hardest part; to ride him. Tommy, as I named this horse, was not going to have any of this nonsense of having a man on his back.

Dad's brother Jim was on holiday with us at this time and he was helping Dad to master this fiery little horse. With one front leg strapped up so that he had only three legs to walk on they could manage to stay in the saddle, but as soon as the tied up front leg was released he would bolt down the paddock and buck them off.

48

After being dumped many times, they tied him up to the post again. After having lunch, they led him up to Greenridge where they rode him on a freshly ploughed paddock. On newly-ploughed ground, it is very hard for a horse to gallop or buck and also it was nice and soft if the rider had a fall. Tommy was ridden home later in the afternoon, soaked in sweat and looking very subdued.

After that, Dad rode him every day until he became quiet and reliable. For many months after that, he always bucked when he was saddled. It was a proud and happy day for me when I was allowed to ride him and he turned out to be a very reliable and hardy little shepherd's hack and a great joy to me, serving me well for many years.

When I was about twelve, Dad went down to North Otago for a holiday. He left me in charge of the horses and the cows. I put Tommy in harness and walked behind him around the horse paddock. I then made a small cart out of some disk wheels and an implement seat. I yoked Tommy to it and drove him round the paddock while sitting in the cart. Mum did not know what I was doing, and when Dad came home, he was shocked. He told me not to do that again. I then realised that it had been quite dangerous.

Helping Dad

Going back to my qualifications at leaving school, I could milk a cow and harness and yoke three horses in a dray using a box to stand on to do up the buckles on the collars and hanes. I wasn't very tall when I finished school at 13 years of age, but like all country boys of that time, was well used to being around horses.

I was used to driving a horse in a gig or dray from quite a young age. When I was still going to school, I had driven Gordie in the dray around to Craigmore Settlement one Saturday to get six bags of seed oats for Dad from a Mr Irvine who farmed over there. Alan Margaret and Alister accompanied me on that 12-mile trip, which took us most of the day. Another time, I drove our six-horse team pulling a grubber preparing the ground for wheat, while Dad trimmed the gorse hedge in the same paddock. I thought I was quite skilled, but of course, I wasn't.

That first year home on the farm began as a very happy time for me, as I loved working with Dad at whatever task he was engaged in. We spent long days carting chaff and grain between the two farms; Dad would sing the old Scottish songs as we sat up on the top of the load as the dray rambled along the shingle road. I learnt those songs off by heart too, just by listening to him. He was a happy man, always singing as he worked. I remember him taking me with him to a farm sale in Cattle Valley where he seemed to meet a lot of farmers that he knew and enjoyed having a yarn and a joke with them. He seemed to be popular with all the people he met, and I was proud of him. They were indeed good days for me.

Of course, I spent a lot of time on my own riding around the sheep, bringing home the cows and helping Mum to milk them and separate the milk and feed the calves and pigs. Dad would be away a lot of the time with the team, working long days preparing the land for crops.

I would get the stable ready at night for the horses arriving home. I would put chaff in the feeders and then go out on to the road and listen for the rattle of the harness or Dad singing as the team plodded home with Dad riding one of the team horses. We would take the horses to the river for a drink of water and then back to the stable to remove their harness. We would hang it up on the wall above their heads, as each horse had its own special harness. After tea, we would go out again and give the horses a second feed of chaff and put their covers on ready to be turned out into the night paddock about an hour and a half later.

How I enjoyed those carefree days doing those jobs on the farm, being trusted to look after the sheep out on the riverbed. To me, this was really living. I was old enough to think I was a man, but still young enough to enjoy simple fun with the rest of the family; life wasn't all work and no play. Helen was at home helping Mum in the house, so this made things easier for her and she was able to spend more time in the garden and milking the cows, a task that she liked. She always said that sitting milking a cow was restful. Dad was a big strong man, probably about 15 stone in weight, and this gave me a great sense of security.

Drought

But there were things happening that I was too young to realise. A financial depression was spreading across the world and by 1930-31, this was really beginning to have a serious effect on the economy of N.Z. Also, in Canterbury, a drought was holding the farm lands in a very tight grip. There had been very little rain over the autumn and winter and by spring pastures were very parched and water for livestock was in very short supply.

I recall that somewhere about the end of Oct 1931 that Dad brought most of the ewes and lambs down from Greenridge and turned them out on to the "riverbed" because the dams on Greenridge had run empty.

As Dad and Mum let the sheep out the gate, a southerly blew up and it started to drizzle, and they stood looking at the sky wondering if they were doing the wrong thing. Was the much-needed rain coming? No, the rain was not coming, the clouds soon dispersed and the sun was shining again.

There was plenty of drinking water in the "riverbed" even though later the river would stop running; there were springs, swamps, and small lagoons. One across the road from the "Parira" home was large enough to row a small boat on. The extra sheep would put pressure on the feed available as it was already stocked with its usual complement of sheep, plus the cows, some young cattle and the horses when they were not working.

There was a great variety of edible plants around a river. Animals loved the leaves and bark of the willow trees and grass grew in the shade of willows even at times of extreme drought. There were also water weeds. I have seen sheep wading in the water halfway up their sides eating watercress and mint and other weeds. Even the green shoots of gorse were freely eaten by hungry sheep.

Worry

I know now, looking back with the knowledge of adulthood, that our parents were probably very worried at that time, with the prospect of falling prices for all farm products, poor returns from sheep as they produced less wool and small lambs through not having enough to eat, and on top of that, the failure of the crops from lack of moisture. I, of course, was too young and inexperienced to notice what was really happening. I was quite oblivious to the fact that my parents and neighbours were living in a real crisis.

I remember one day Dad was out by the shed painting a dray, when Jack Martin, who was riding past stopped for a yarn. When he remarked about the painting work, Dad laughed and said he might have to have a "clearing sale".

This was the way that mercantile firms dealt with farmers who could not pay their debts. As he faced each day with the burning sun, the howling norwesters and the stunted crops maybe this was a very real thought in his mind. Whether this was the way he was thinking or not we will never know, but as time went on, I noticed a change coming over him, he seemed to have become quiet and was no longer the jovial person I had known.

When we went out to the stable at night to tend to the horses, he would go and lean over the rails on the fence around the stable yard seemingly deep in thought, not speaking. I knew in my heart something was very wrong that I didn't understand; I was frightened. I found it difficult being alone with him and I feared for him when I wasn't there.

Farming with Mum

Dad's Death

On a Sunday morning in November 1931, we boys were having fun in our bedroom, as we never got up early on a Sunday morning. Mum came in and asked me to go and get the cows in, as Dad wasn't feeling well and had gone out to the toilet. I ran away out through the yard, but when I got to the gate by the fowl-house, there was Dad lying dead, with the gun lying alongside him. What a shock, the bottom dropped out of my world.

I turned and raced back to the house for Mum. I don't remember much about the rest of that awful day—my mind is a blank. I guess I was suffering from shock. I know Mum rang for Mr Gainsford who arrived quickly and they phoned for the police who were soon on the scene. Uncle Alex came over from Hazelburn and later in the morning, he and I milked the cows. I guess Uncle Bob would be there too, but I do not remember.

Dad's funeral was held in our house, conducted by old Mr Morton who was the minister at Albury. I don't remember anything about that either except that Mr Morton took me out into the garden. The only thing I remember him saying to me was, "Boy, be good to your mother". I never forgot those words and as long as Mum was alive, I honestly tried to carry them out.

Mum's determination

Life has to go on, and this was a new era for the McKenzie family, a family without a father, now headed by a mother who was determined to succeed, to keep her family together and to provide them with food, clothing and an example in how to live.

Mum would have been only forty years old, quite a small woman, but she seemed to have tremendous strength and ability to work. I suppose in the years that followed, she seemed to be a fairly serious person, but these were serious times. I think that in her young days she would be a fun-loving person. She was a good dancer, easy to dance with, proficient on the piano and organ, a good cook, baker, and dressmaker.

How Mum got through those days, I don't know, but I know this that never for one minute did she neglect us children. It seems to me from my sketchy memory that she got straight down to being both Mum and Dad to her family. Looking back, one can imagine the sadness, grief and fear she must have experienced, but she hid it from me, and I suppose too from the rest of the family.

Even though Mum was a small woman, she was very strong emotionally with a deep faith in God as her protector and guide. I don't think I ever doubted that she would get us safely through those difficult days of December 1931 and the years that followed. At the beginning of her diary for 1935, she wrote:

> As we start another year, we feel we have much to be
> thankful for and trust that God will be with us each day in
> the year we are entering.

At meal times, Dad had sat at one end of the table in a large chair (that I later had at Parira). Mum sat at the other end of the table close to the kitchen. The boys sat at the back of the table against the wall, and the girls sat on the other side. When Dad died, Mum moved me into Dad's chair and gave me his cup. It was a big one that he had bought at an Exhibition in Christchurch. Sitting in Dad's chair made me feel really responsible for the rest of the family.

Good Neighbours

Mr Gainsford was a wonderful neighbour to us for the next few years. Quite soon after Dad's death, he and Mr Cooper came one day with their teams and sowed rape and turnips on the ground that Dad had prepared, but owing to the fact that it did not rain, the crops they sowed were a failure, and only weeds grew.

Mr Gainsford and Dad had always worked together in the seasonal work of shearing, harvesting, tailing etc. It seems as though he just carried on helping Mum by working with me in getting those jobs done. Looking back now, I realise what a patient, good-hearted man he was because he was no longer working with a neighbour who could pull his weight, but with an inexperienced boy. I don't remember him ever being impatient, even though he must have been doing the lion's share of the work. Mr Gainsford was a very good farmer and a good living man, a very good example for a boy to learn from and to follow.

Mum employed Eddy Kelynack a neighbour's son to help with that season's harvest, though because of the drought, the crops were very short and light. Eddy and I did the reaping and stooking and Mr Gainsford helped with the stacking, he being a very competent stacker and able to cope with the very short sheaves from the stunted, drought-stricken crops. We had four small stacks of wheat and three of oats. The wheat threshed about 20 bushels to the acre, about half of what one would expect in a normal year.

This was better than for many people; their crops had been grazed by hungry sheep, as they were too stunted to reap. I remember helping Mr Gainsford with his wheat, my job being to rake up the loose straw along the rows of stooks with a hand rake, it was so short that sheaves fell to pieces. It was very difficult to stack and the end result was about 10 bushels an acre.

Floods

Towards the end of February, the harvest was only just finished when the rain came, but this turned out to be a disaster for us too. I didn't have enough experience to know what to do when the drought broke and the river began to run again. With most of the ewes and their lambs out on the riverbed because of the available water, they were at great risk from a major flood. The rain had started to fall in the afternoon and through the night it just teemed down. When we went out in the morning, the river was in high flood and it was too late to do anything about the sheep, which should have been mustered off before the river rose too high.

Some neighbours came in the morning and tried to shift some of the sheep, but it was hopeless, as there was water everywhere. Looking from the "Riverbank" house, which was close to the river,

Rod at Riverbank

but several feet above the highest flood level, one couldn't even imagine how any sheep could survive in the raging flood that seemed to cover the whole area. But somehow, survive they did, as when the flood subsided and we were able to muster the sheep, we were amazed how small the losses were. We didn't know for certain how many sheep Dad had out there, but by the number that were mustered, we knew the losses were very light.

The flood was said to be the biggest on record. There was tremendous damage done to bridges, roads, and fencing, the approach to the Cliff Bridge was washed out and the main floodwaters by-passed the Martin's Crossing bridge, most of the water flowing on the north side of the bridge.

For the first time, the main stream had shifted from the north side to the south bank and became a real threat at each following flood. Even small ones would erode more of the freehold land that was used for cropping, and of course each time, the fences would be washed away as well. This was before the days of bulldozers when the course of a river could be changed and good land protected.

One could only stand by and watch helplessly as the land disappeared downstream in the floodwaters.

It wasn't until many years later when Alister owned "Riverbank", when a programme guided and subsidised by the Catchment Board was put into action, that the land was made safe and the erosion stopped. Big willow branches secured by wire ropes were placed along the banks and stop banks built by bulldozers.

Repairing Fences

On the "Riverbank" farm the damage to fences was considerable, as there wasn't a paddock that didn't have some of its fences washed away, and quite a lot of land washed away too. To get the fences replaced and the farm stock-proof again, I was helped by George Weavers, a neighbour's son, who hadn't been left school many years. Uncle Bob arranged for him to help me in this work but he had had little experience in fencing and I had none, so it was the blind leading the blind.

Looking back now I am amazed at the small amount of practical help given by our uncles. Uncle Alex Wisley was retired in Timaru, having retired from farming before he was 50 and Alex McKenzie seemed to be semi-retired living in the school house at Hazelburn.

I don't remember either of them giving any advice or practical help. Perhaps we didn't ask for it, or they thought we didn't want their help. But to go back to the repairing of the fences, George and I worked away using retrieved wire and willow stakes (which would only last about two years), putting up fences that were to be a source of trial for many years. However, we did get the fences to the stage where all the paddocks would hold stock again and boundary fences reasonably secure.

Tough Year

At that time, the farm was under the control of Public Trust, as executors of the will that Dad made with them. While I don't remember them as being very helpful, nor do I remember them being a hindrance in any way. Because it was a poor year financially, there was little money available to buy fencing material, so much time was spent retrieving wire from the fences that were washed away. There did seem to be reluctance by Mum to spend money on anything like fencing material, so we struggled away with what was available. I can understand this. The depression, drought, flood, very low returns for farm products and the news of farmers being "sold up" put a real fear of overspending into the thinking of most people.

That period from November 1931 into the autumn of 1932 was indeed a disaster time. The rape and turnips that our neighbours had kindly sown for us failed to grow, because of the drought, so there was no rape to fatten the lambs on and no turnips for winter feed for the ewes. There was only going to be about half the chaff needed to feed a team of working horses until next harvest, so it was a pretty grim picture.

Selling Lambs

I can't remember much of what happened during the first few months following Dad's death, as my mind is a blank, but I do remember the lambs being sold. After the havoc of the flood was behind us, we mustered the sheep off the riverbed and weaned the lambs and put them up on Greenridge where there was a tremendous growth of grass following the long period of drought.

Alister, Alan & Rod

However, they had to be sold, as there was no rape to fatten them.

I remember bringing them home to be inspected by our fat lamb buyer Mr Hutton. He apparently didn't expect any of the lambs to be fat, as he had brought a sheep dealer with him. After inspecting the lambs and agreeing that none were suitable for the freezing works, the

58

dealer Mr Sheehan made an offer of 10 shillings for them as stores. Remembering that fat lambs had been selling for nearly 30 shillings in the late 1920s, this seemed a very poor price.

Uncle Bob was present to advise Mum and he said, "No you can't sell them for that low price". I am not sure what he thought we were going to do with them. I let the lambs out on the road to go back to Greenridge. As soon as Uncle Bob had gone, Mr Hutton said, "Mrs McKenzie, I think you are making a very serious mistake, that is a very good offer". Mum asked me to bring the lambs back and she sold them for 10 shillings.

That was a good lesson for me, not to hold on to stock when you don't have feed for them. It was the first time that I had anything to do with selling stock. I learnt that day to never turn down a good offer and also that there were men in the trade that you could trust. Mr Hutton was a good friend to our family for many years. (Sims Cooper also gained a loyal client that day.) A few weeks later, fat lambs were being sold for 8 shillings.

With the lambs sold and away off the farm and the wheat and wool sold, Mum would now know what the income from farm produce was and what funds she had available to pay farm expenses and provide for family needs until about March 1933.

Bill Giles

There is no diary available for 1932, and my memory is a bit rusty, but sometime in the autumn of 1932, on the advice of Mr Crawford's teamster, Mum employed a young man Bill Giles to be teamster and do the agricultural work. He suggested Bill because he was a friend of the family. Mr Griffin, who farmed what we later called "Griffin's block", had married Mrs Giles and Bill was her son.

Looking back now that wasn't a very wise move, as Bill was about 18 or 19 years old and had very little experience in the work he was given to do. Mum expected Mr Crawford's teamster to keep an eye on him, but he didn't. Maybe a more experienced man would have been a better proposition in the long run. I know that he and I between us we made a lot of mistakes that a more experienced man would not have made.

I presume that Mum would want someone who would fit in with the family, as the only accommodation was the spare room in the house. Bill met the requirements in that area, because he was good-natured and easy to get on with. He was able to drive the car and take the family to church on Sundays. He also took Helen and me to dances and parties and also to Bible Class meetings.

Bill loved to go out at night. He would visit neighbours to play cards most nights of the week, so he was very difficult to wake up in the morning. Some mornings Mum would almost break the wall down, banging her hands on it trying to wake him up, but being a peace-loving, good-natured person she seemed to be prepared to put up with it.

I enjoyed having Bill around, finding him good company. I saw him as very much a man of the world and much more experienced in that area than I was. As time went on, even my inexperienced eyes could see that he was not a good hand with horses and very slow at getting through the work with the team. I should note that he was not getting paid very much, only 15 shillings a week ($1-50).

One day we were driving the team, the horses stopped on the road. He started to yank at the reins. I said to him, "That is not the way to treat horses". He was annoyed and said, "You drive them then", so I did. That night he handed in his notice.

Learning Stock Management Skills
While Bill wasn't doing very well finding his way as a teamster, I probably wasn't doing much better in caring for the sheep. You will remember I had only had one year home on the farm, so I was no way prepared to take charge of a flock of sheep, but I relished the responsibility and was full of enthusiasm.

Our neighbour Mr Crawford was very good at teaching me the skills of shepherding and sheep handling. Any time that the sheep had to be sorted for tupping, mouthed for culling or ewe lambs selected for replacements, he would be present to help. He did this for several years, and I learnt a lot from him, as he was probably the most successful Romney sheep breeder in the district at that time. Dad had always bought in ewes for replacements, but Mum made the change to breeding our own replacements. It was a much safer way to farm, not being at the mercy of the markets.

Stock wise, we were facing a very difficult winter as the drought caused the turnip crop to be a total failure. There wasn't enough oaten chaff for the horses, let alone any to spare for the sheep. This was before the days of making hay for sheep feed. The cattle scraped through on a few mangolds and wheat straw. To overcome this feed problem and to keep the sheep alive till the spring came, Mum appealed to Peter McPherson, who was an old school mate of Dad's. He was now the local stock agent, so he made arrangements for us to buy turnips for grazing at Sutherlands, about eighteen miles away. From memory, I think the turnips cost 1/- (10c) a sheep.

The sheep were to be driven by road, taking two days. I was all for doing the job myself, but after consulting Uncle Bob, Mum wouldn't let me do it alone, so Helen came with me on the first day to Cave. We left the sheep in the sale yards and the next day cousin Alex came with me on the rest of the journey.

About two months later, Alex and I brought them home again in time for lambing. I was excited about that venture. It was big stuff for me driving sheep out on the open road. This was the sort of thing I dreamed about since a little boy, being a shepherd in charge of a flock of sheep. I had my horse and Dad's two dogs. I was growing up fast, so I thought.

Dogs

Dad had two dogs Roy and Rover. Roy was useless and did not do much, but Rover was quite useful. They were never tied up and would often be fighting. Dad used to kill a sheep under a willow tree down the bank. In those days, there were no concerns about hydatids, so the offal was just thrown aside for the dogs to eat. Whenever Dad killed a sheep, the smell of blood would set them fighting. They would fight until they were exhausted.

I was quite proud of having a dog that was a good fighter, until one day I was coming down the road and met Jack Martin coming up the road in his gig on his way to get some sheep. He was an Irishman who lived with Mrs Weavers and was the local drover. As he passed, Rover attacked one of his dogs, and we had to stop them. Jack really told me off. He said that his dogs were his livelihood and he could not afford to lose them. I was a bit put out at first, but later I realised that he was right. This was a good lesson for me, and I resolved never to let any dog that belonged to me to get into a fight.

Droving Sheep

About a year after Dad died, we had some sheep to sell in the sale at Pleasant Point. Mum talked with Uncle Bob, and he contacted Jack Martin. Each Sunday, he would gather up a flock of sheep from all over the district to take down to the Point sale. Sometimes he would have sheep and cattle together. He told Uncle Bob that it would cost 10 shillings. Uncle Bob told Mum that this was too expensive and that she should get the boy to take them down to Point.

On the next Saturday, I drove the sheep over to Cave and put them in the sheepyards by the railway. Sunday was an absolutely terrible day. As I was going over to Cave to take the sheep on to Point, I met Jack Martin coming back the other way. He said that he was going home to get covers for his horses, because it was so cold. He said that I should go home too. "Don't worry about your sheep", he said, "I will get them down to the sale". He did not charge us anything. I was really grateful for his help.

First Lambing

I don't remember much about that first lambing that I had responsibility for, but I do remember finding lambs dead in the morning. I didn't know that I should be going around the ewes several times a day during the lambing season. However, I soon learnt from experience and by observing what other farmers did. There was no school for young shepherds, and many changes were taking place in sheep farming in the early 1930s. However, we did get safely through 1932, and I note that Mum wrote at the beginning of her 1933 diary that the shearing had been completed on Dec 19 1932, with 475 sheep being shorn. No doubt, Mr Gainsford had provided guidance.

The early shearers were Jack Martin and Pat Casey. They used to make a holiday of it and would only shear about 150 sheep between them each day. Mr Gainsford had to use them because his daughter was married to Pat. We used his woolshed, so we had to use his shearers.

Mum got really frustrated with them. Jack had been a good shearer, but when working with Pat, he seemed to take things easy. Later when the war came, and he was in his late forties, he went out with an old mate and they worked seven days a week, shearing about 200 a day each. Later, Alister and I started doing the shearing ourselves.

Trusting God

At the beginning of that 1933 diary Mum wrote, "Prices for all stock have never been lower, wool realised £6 a bale at the December sale, lambs 4½ pence a lb, butter 5 pence". She continued with the words, "We trust in the coming year that God will help us from day to day and that the depression will be followed by a year of happiness and prosperity". I believe that Mum's faith in God enabled her to get through those difficult days with confidence.

Haymaking

I notice too that in early January, both Bill and I spent quite a lot of time helping Mr Gainsford to make hay. One day Bill was driving Mr Gainsford's team for him, so I guess we did return some of the favours he had given us. I remember that haymaking well. I had the job of raking the hay, using our horse Gordie to pull the hay rake. Gordie was a big slow horse and I was offended when one of the men came out to me and asked me if I could put on a bigger cog. I wasn't sure what he meant, but learnt later that he was telling me to go a bit faster, as I wasn't helping on the stack.

Another little incident that comes to mind was losing the new jersey that I was wearing at that time. In the heat of the day, I had taken it off and placed alongside the stack for safety, not realising that as a stack grew higher, the weight caused it to spread out. So when I went to get it at night, it was nowhere to be found. It was buried under the stack. In the following winter, Mr Gainsford found it when he was feeding out the hay, but unfortunately, he had cut the sleeve off with his hay knife. All good experience.

Dipping

Time was also spent in dipping and weaning lambs, just under 100% of lambs weaned, 51 going to the works fat off the mothers. The water for the dip had to be carted in a 200-gallon tank on the dray, the tank being filled by driving the horse into deep water and filling the tank with a bucket. This was a continuing task as each sheep would take out about 1/2 a gallon of water in its wool. Mr Gainsford and Mr Priest also dipped their sheep in our dip.

Social Activities

As I have said earlier that there is no diary available for 1932, but notes in Mums 1933 diary show that as a family, we were back into the swing of district social activities. We were attending church at St Davids, Cave every Sunday and Bible Class during the week. Mum was active in the Women's Division of Federated Farmers, being a committee member. These meetings were held in the school and to attend she either walked or rode the old bike. She was often visiting or being visited by neighbours. Helen was attending Women's Institute meetings and picnics sometimes accompanied by Margaret. Helen and I were going to dances and socials in the Cave hall and Cannington School. I had my driver's license by this time and Mum placed no restrictions on us using the car, as long as we behaved ourselves.

I can see now that Mum allowing and encouraging us to take part in district activities had been good for us and speeded the healing process from the stress of losing our Dad.

Alister, Rod and Uncle Jack

Although I wasn't aware of it at the time, I can see now that she used great wisdom in this area. It must have been very hard for her considering the grief and stress she was bearing at the time. I remember too, that for the younger members of the family, more activities were taking place at the school. For example, sports days were being held, where the pupils competed against the Cave school in football and basketball.

Sport

I often wondered in later life why I wasn't very interested in sport, but I now realise that there were no sports of any kind while I was at school. The only exception was a little basketball that the teacher tried to involve the whole school in, but the older boys considered that this was a girls' game and beneath their dignity. So, we were unwilling to take part and became disruptive players and also losers. There was no football at school until I was in Standard 5, and this was given to the school by a Catholic priest, who used to visit the school to give religious education to the Catholic boys.

We had a woman teacher who seldom came out into the playground, so no organised sport took place. We boys left school quite ignorant of New Zealand's national game. I can see now that when I left school, my aims and desires were not towards sport, but leaned towards the pleasure of achieving in the field of work; I was quite unaware that I was missing anything. With the arrival of a male teacher at the school, this was all changed. It meant that by the time Alister was in the upper classes, he was playing rugby in school and outside.

The Slump

Many things were taking place in the district that were to have an influence on our later lives. An example is the radio that we got in 1936. This brought the outside world right into our home. I think this might have been partly financed by a gift from Aunt Bessie.

The "selling up" of farmers was taking place as banks and mercantile firms were foreclosing on farmers who owed them money. The first I remember was Harry Webb in the Craigmore soldier settlement. Uncle Bob had taken me to the sale. I remember Mr Webb, standing before the farmers gathered for the sale, bitterly declaring that the nation had been pleased with him when he went overseas to fight in the 1914-18 war, but now when he was fighting for his survival financially, they seemed to have forgotten about him. He was quickly shut up, and the sale went on. Uncle Bob bought some good four- and five-year old ewes for us for 7/- (70c), a bargain price.

The next sale was also for a returned serviceman, Chris Cooper, who was a widower with five children. His land was across the road from ours, a half a mile down the road. Twice earlier, the sale had been cancelled by pressure by members of the Farmers Union, but this time there was no stopping it. Chris and his five children walked off to go and live in an empty farm cottage belonging to a farmer friend. Some years later, I met Chris in town where he worked as a cleaner in the Timaru Post Office.

His farm was bought by Jim and Ian Calder and their coming into the district was to have an impact on my life. They were great horse and dog men, and I saw for the first time well-trained sheepdogs. It was Jim who introduced me to mustering on hill country, an occupation that was a real joy to me.

The next sale to have an impact on me was our neighbour up the road Doxon Priest. He was an older man and went to live in a friend's farm cottage; he died of cancer a few years later. Across the river, Len Marshall met the same fate. Next door to him, Dick Williams and Joe Scott lost the farm we knew as "Dockerty's". Next year, Dick, an old grey-haired man, crutched some of our sheep for 5/- shillings a hundred.

These were our neighbours, who farmed in a circle around us, so this had an impact on my way of thinking. I made up my mind, that if I achieved my dream to have a farm of my own, I would never get into debt to a bank or mercantile firm.

Harvest

Life was not all doom and gloom. I don't suppose the younger members of the family even noticed that these things were happening. I would imagine that for them, things would seem quite normal. Alan, Margaret and Alister were busy at school, doing the things that school children do from day to day. Helen was helping Mum in the house, learning the skills of house-keeping. I was learning new skills in farm work.

Bill and I learned together how to operate a reaper and binder as the crops were harvested. I learned to stook the sheaves of oats and wheat, under the watchful eye of Cyril Guthrie, a man from Albury, who had lost

Alan Stooking

his farm through the depression. There was a real skill in getting 10 or 12 sheaves to stand up in the form of a stook, so that the rain would run off and the straw would dry and the grain mature. Also, the stook had to be put up in a way, that it could stand up to norwest gales, so as to avoid the unpleasant task of re-stooking after a big wind. There was a real feeling of satisfaction as the last sheaf was picked up and one looked across a paddock of straight rows of stooks.

The crop would remain like that for about 2 weeks until it was ready to stack. The stacking was done by a gang of 5 men with two drays. We were working with Mr Gainsford and Mr Cooper, so the crops on three farms had to be stacked in turn over a period of several weeks.

This was a busy time for the house as well, as all meals were eaten in the paddock. Besides morning and afternoon teas, a hot dinner had to be packed and brought out to the paddock where the stacking was being done. Mrs Gainsford brought theirs out in a horse and sledge. Helen and Mum would bring ours out in the gig pulled by Gypsy Grey.

Those picnic lunches were a pleasant respite in a long busy day, as work would often go on until darkness came on at night, but they meant long and busy days for the women. It seemed to be a never-ending cycle, as no sooner was the harvest finished, than it was time to start ploughing for the next lot of crops.

Rabbits

The rabbit problem was becoming real in those days and for the first time, we started laying poison on the riverbed, where rabbit numbers were growing. The first time we used phosphorous poison, but it was not very effective, so in later years we used strychnine, which was much more effective. I think the biggest kill on the riverbed was about 500 rabbits. It is said that 7 rabbits ate as much grass as one sheep, so the rabbit menace was a real threat to our well-being. This problem continued for a number of years, until rabbit boards were formed and a concentrated effort was made to exterminate this destructive pest. This was never achieved, but numbers were kept down to a level where they were not a menace.

We children were always trapping rabbits, so on a winter's night after dark, a lighted lantern would be seen bobbing around amongst the gorse bushes as the McKenzie children went around their traps, before they went to bed. This night trip was done to avoid cruelty to the poor rabbit and to avoid finding a sprung trap with only a rabbit's foot left in the trap on the morning round. Even Margaret took part in this activity.

Once Alan and I took a bag of about twenty or thirty skins into the dealer in Timaru. He said to us, "What a shame! The market has absolutely gone to pieces." He offered a very low price and told us he was being very generous. Alan and I swallowed the story and sold him the skins for a few pence. When Mum found out, she was absolutely disgusted that he had taken advantage of two young boys, but there was nothing we could do.

Killing a Pig

That year too, I learnt how to kill a pig, a task I never enjoyed, especially in those early days before a rifle was used. Can you picture me standing astride a big pig holding its two front legs and keeping it on its back, the pig squealing like a mad thing and me trying to hold it still while Mr Gainsford plunged a knife into the pig's throat area, allowing it to bleed to death? Sometimes the knife would touch the heart and this would cause it to die quicker.

Each farm would kill two or three pigs each year, to provide bacon and ham. After the killing (this was called "sticking", hence the term "bled like a stuck pig") the pig was put in a wooden trough in which boiling water had been poured. It would be turned over and over until the hair came off easily. Then it would be taken out and scraped clean with a sharp knife and hung up to set overnight.

Next day, it would be sawn down the centre of the backbone and each side cut into three pieces. The rib bones cut out (called pork bones) were roasted and eaten. Roasted pork bones were looked upon as a treat. The pieces left were placed in a tub and sprinkled with salt. The meat gradually absorbed the salt. This process was called "being cured". Once it was "cured", it became bacon or ham and it was hung up, to be used for breakfast over the months ahead. In later years this "curing" process was taken over by professionals in town, making it much easier to "bring home the bacon".

A common sight in many farm kitchens was sides of bacon and hams hanging from hooks in the ceiling. It was important that boys growing up on a farm learnt the skills of killing and processing animals for food. We learnt by observing how our elders did it.

There were a lot of dealers in those days for rabbit skins and sheep skins. They would travel around the district and buy from the farmers. They were all pretty sharp. Some would buy fat, I presume for making soap. When we killed a sheep or pig, Mum would take all the fat from around the stomach and the kidneys and render it into a kerosene tin. The fat buyers would carry a metal spear, that they would poke into the tin of fat to check that it was not solid. Sometimes, they would find a sheep's head or something that someone had put in to increase the bulk. A four-gallon tin of fat would be worth about five shillings.

Preserving Meat

Providing and storing meat for the family and workers throughout the year was time-consuming work for the housewife. In the summer season, mutton would often be salted, "pickled," to keep it from going bad in the hot weather. Like most farmers, we were big meat eaters, mostly having meat three times a day. Bacon or chops for breakfast, hot roast mutton at midday and cold meat again for tea in the evening. There would also be potatoes three times a day, fried for breakfast and tea and boiled at midday.

Whenever Dad went to town, he would bring home 2/- worth of sausages and 1/6 worth of fish, and we kept that up for many years. It would be only on rare occasions that a farmer would buy anything other than sausages and saveloys from the butcher. Sometimes some beef would be bought, although much of the beef was killed on the farm. A beast killed at the beginning of winter and hung up in a shady tree, would keep for many weeks in the frosty weather.

By the time the beast was finished, we would be absolutely sick of eating beef and would be pleased to get back on to mutton again. Like most farmers, we were very much mutton eaters.

This preserving and storing of meat was all changed with the coming of the freezer and fridge, but in spite of the lack of these modern amenities, we never were short of food. That was one of the blessings of being on a farm in hard times. There was always plenty of food. There wasn't much money, but as children, we had no need for it, because we weren't going anywhere to spend money. Our fun and enjoyment had to be created in the family amongst ourselves.

Improving Prices

1934 brought some good things and some disappointments. Mum began the diary that year by noting that wool prices had risen 100%. The price of wool was 9 pence to 19 pence per pound. Lamb was 7¼ pence per pound and butterfat 7 pence. These were still very poor prices, but the corner was turned and prices were going up. On the same page, Mum gave thanks to God for his protection over the past year and expressed her trust for the year ahead.

Church

Mum placed great importance on going to church. When she employed a man to work the team, she stipulated that he had to be willing to drive the car and take us to church on Sunday. I remember one day when Bill was away for some reason and was not able to take us to church, Mum made us get out the horse and gig so we could still go.

Dad went to church too, but I don't think there was much Christianity in his family. Granny did not go to church much, although Mum did try to get her to go. She had become bitter and blamed God for Dad's death.

We only started going to church at Cave in 1928, when the St Davids church opened. Before that time Church was held at the Cannington School. We were part of the Albury parish and the minister would come once a fortnight to a service at the school. About twenty families would attend and the children would sit at the school desks. There were also two big long forms that the church had brought. By the time the church moved, they were pretty well wrecked. People were quite happy when the church stopped meeting at the Cannington School. They were glad to get out of the school into a church.

The leading men in the church were Mr Crawford and Mr Brown from Cave. They were fairly old-fashioned services. Mum played the piano for the singing of hymns. She was the first organist at the Cave church. There was no Sunday School.

I can still remember sitting and looking at the maps on the wall. I did not understand much of what the minister was talking about. I must have got something, because when Dad died, I started to pray. I didn't really know how to pray, so I would sing hymns, but putting my own words to them. I would sing out loud, if I were outside in the paddocks. As I rode around the sheep, I would sing,

> Jesus loves me, this I know
> For the Bible tells me so
> If I love him while I ride
> He will stay right by my side.

Not having a father telling me how to do things, I used to pray a lot. I had to learn by watching other people, so I used to pray that I would find the right help.

The minister at the time of Dad's death was Mr Morton. He was an old man, who had come from Milton, where Mum had known him in her younger days. He was a lovely old man. All he asked for when he came to the parish, was a horse and gig. He drove all over the parish visiting the people.

Neighbours

Mr Gainsford

In 1934, our best neighbour Mr Gainsford sold his farm and moved away. He was quite an old man and had been trying to sell for a number of years. He was a good farmer, with good stock, good horses and good equipment. He had a good car and was one of the first in the district to have a radio.

Mr Gainsford helped to milk the cows while attending school in Christchurch. After leaving school, he worked on farms in North Canterbury. He first took up land near Hawarden, where he ran sheep and grew crops. He married Mary Hogben of Masons Flat. When the Motukaika was being cut up by Messrs Belcher and Chapman in 1906, he purchased the farm that would become Parira.

Mr Gainsford wasn't very well rewarded for the years of work. He bought the bare land in 1906 for £10 an acre. He came in a horse and dray and put up a tent in the corner on the site of the current house. He lived in the tent while he built a shed over it. He later built three rooms of the house. Over the years he completed the house and sheds, put up fences and dug wells for water. He sold the farm for £13 10/- an acre in 1935.

His clearing sale showed the new hope farmers had. The price of horses boomed to £60 for the best, displaying a belief that farming had a future. I had been fortunate in having such a good farmer and a good man to guide me in those difficult years, but it was also good for me to have to stand on my own feet.

Doxon Priest

Mr Priest also had to leave his farm in 1934, being sold up by Dalgety. He went away broken financially and healthwise and only lived a few more years. He had told me that he never had enough money. He was always short, even after he sold off 400 acres to Pat Casey and Dad.

He may not have been cut out to be a farmer. He was great at running the school and doing that kind of thing. When electricity came around, he put it in all his sheds. He milked a lot of cows, but he did not seem to be so good at managing sheep.

We missed the Priests, as we had gone to school with their seven children and they had been good neighbours. Their farm was bought for the price of the mortgage on it (£11 an acre) by Mr Crawford for his son Norman. This was the beginning of a life-long friendship, which is still going on today.

We reaped the benefit of the high price for horses, as we sold old Gordie for £24. A hack that had been a bit of an outlaw, that Dad had broken in to work in the team, sold for £5. We had three young horses broken in that year by an expert horse breaker giving me the chance to learn a new way of handling unbroken horses. This was a skill that stood both Alister and me in good stead.

The Riverbed

Mum had a lot of difficulty with Mr Kelynack over the lease of the riverbed. He believed that he owned the little piece of land between the fence and the river. Grandad did not like him, so I presume that they had disagreed over the same issue.

Mr Kelynack's claim was unfounded, as the boundary of his farm was the old Levels station fence that was still in place. The piece of land he claimed was on our side of the only fence, so there was nothing to keep his sheep from getting mixed up with our sheep. When he put his sheep out on this piece of land, they would cross the river to our side. He would then upset Mum by phoning her and demanding to get his sheep back.

It seemed to her to become quite an obsession with him. Once Len Marshall who owned the farm next to him had bought a lot of Merino wethers up at Burkes Pass.

When it got dry, he ran out of feed for them. I went over the river and found the boundary fence had been taken down and all the wethers were grazing in the riverbed. Len explained to me that Mr Kelynack had told him he could do it. Soon after, Len Marshall had a breakdown and ended up in hospital. Sid Kelynack, who was looking after the farm, helped me to restore the fence.

I got tired of Mr Kelynack upsetting Mum, so I told him to phone me if he had any problems. I asked how many sheep the disputed land could carry. He said two ewes and their lambs. I suggested that they would earn him £4, so I agreed to pay him £4 a year, if he kept his sheep inside the fence. Mum really begrudged paying the money for land that was ours, but it was worth it for the peace. We paid that £4 every year until Alister took over the farm and stopped it. By then Mr Kelynack was dead.

Many years later, Mr Kelynack told me that he had been offended by the way that I spoke to him. When Keith Crawford bought Mr Kelynack's farm years later, he measured the property and found that the fence was in the correct place.

Gerald Casey

During the drought, when I was checking the sheep up at Greenridge, another neighbour Gerald Casey came over and complained that 150 of our sheep had got through the fence and ruined his wheat. There were not that many sheep up there, as Dad had brought all the sheep down to Riverbank and he had only taken 80 back up.

Gerald seemed to be really angry. He was jabbing his pitchfork into the ground and speaking loudly. I stayed on my horse, so I could get away if he started to threaten me.

He seemed to make the boundary fence my responsibility. He was always getting me to fix holes in the gorse fence. He also claimed that the boundary fence was three yards too far down the hill and that we had some of his land.

I was really quite frightened of him. If I was going to go back home through Mr Gainsford's flats, and I saw Gerald Casey, I would turn around and ride the long way, down Galways Road, so that I did not have to meet him.

Funnily enough, when he got older, I ended up doing a lot to help him. I would castrate calves and do other things that he could not manage. When he sold the farm to Bill Wright, I helped him to muster his sheep off the farm.

Strong Family

Working Together

In 1934, we had a fall of snow that winter with a lot of frozen and burst pipes. That meant some days of discomfort with no water and not much fire, because of the danger of the cylinder boiling dry as no water would run in. The good side was that we learnt how to cover water pipes against hard frosts and how to mend them when they burst.

I notice in the diary that Alan and Alister started planting trees on spare corners of ground and that Margaret was also out helping on the farm. As I read over those 1934-5 diaries, it is plain that every member of the family was playing their part in the work of the farm, home and garden. With Helen doing a big part of the housework, Mum was spending more time outside in the garden and out in the paddock hoeing mangolds and potatoes. She also milked 5 or 6 cows.

Children grew up useful in those days, and each of the family was capable of taking a horse and dog and going up to Greenridge to bring home a mob of sheep. They generally worked in pairs, it might be Alan and Alister, or Alan and Margaret, away for a mob of sheep, while I was busy with the team or in the shearing shed.

I notice that Alan had taken the hacks to the blacksmith at Cave to have their feet shod, quite a responsibility for a boy of 11 or 12 years. Alister and I got on really well together, as we were both interested in horses and dogs. People called him "my shadow" because he always followed me around.

I record these things so that you the reader will see that the well-being of the McKenzies depended on the co-operation and help of each family member. As far as I can remember, this was all done in a good spirit, although some members may have felt locked into a situation that they had little control over. Looking back, it is a shame that Helen didn't get more education and take up nursing as I think she probably would have liked to. It was the custom in those days for the oldest daughter to stay and help in the home.

Margaret at Greenridge

Helen loved to go out. She went to Red Cross and CWI at Cave and to WDFF at Cannington. She was very strong. She would ride seven miles on a bike to Cave. The road was shingle, and she had to go over the hill, but that did not discourage her. She would walk two miles to the Cannington School. Margaret was not as strong and tended to stay at home.

New Government

1935 brought a change of Government, the tired old conservative government went out and Labour, full of enthusiasm and new ideas, came in and made big changes. They brought in a welfare system and provided work for unemployed men by building new roads and bridges. My friends didn't have much faith in a Labour government, so on someone's advice, I drew my savings out of the Post Office savings bank and transferred them to the National

Bank, believing that because the National Bank was part British, my money would be safer.

I notice that at the end of 1935, we sold some lambs for 22/-; things were coming right. By 1936, there was a new confidence spreading over New Zealand and it was affecting all of our lives.

Mr Semple, a Minister of Works, offended the Tory supporters by driving a bulldozer over the top of a wheelbarrow and shovel as a symbol of the new way. That was the beginning of bulldozers on our roads.

Family Changes

In 1936 Alister and I went for a trip to Christchurch, a big deal. We went up by train on Saturday and stayed at the People's Palace. We went out to Waipara and spent a night with Mr and Mrs Gainsford. We were home again on Wednesday of the next week. It was a very short holiday, but I wouldn't have wanted to be away for long. I would be wanting to get home to my horses and sheep. Bill Giles had left us at the end of 1934, so I had had a year in charge of the team and I just loved it.

We had made some changes with the team. No more trekking back and forwards to Greenridge from Riverbank. We built some big chaff feeders and left the horses up at Greenridge, where most of the work was done. By giving the horses two sacks of chaff to eat overnight, they didn't need so long to feed in the morning. I would leave home at five in the morning and ride a hack up to Greenridge. While the horses were feeding, I would cook my breakfast in the hut. I would be ready to yoke the team by seven o'clock. We also built a small shed alongside the hut, to store chaff for the horses.

Often Margaret would bring up lunch, especially if Alan or Alister were there too. Mum and Margaret thought nothing of walking cross country to bring us lunch. Those were good days. I loved being able to drive the team, with Alan able to go around the sheep and Alister helping on Saturdays or holidays.

That year, Margaret went off to high school, boarding in town for five days and coming home for weekends. Gwen Blackmore was going too, so we were able to share picking them up at Cave. Mum also started to board the local schoolteacher, first a relieving teacher Miss Brown, then after a few weeks, a permanent teacher named Dan Hopkinson. He was to board with us for several years. Dan came from Temuka and was able to go home at weekends.

Having a male teacher meant that boys were playing football. Alister was playing at Cave and at school tournaments, so at least one member of our family knew something about rugby. It was also good to have Dan in our home as he was a good living man and he did have an influence on my life, even though I didn't really enjoy being out in the paddock with him trying to throw the discus.

Improving Economy

Proof that there was more money about was that in 1936, we changed our car, buying a second-hand Plymouth sedan that had done 14,500 miles. It cost £155, less £20 for the trade-in of the model T Ford. We thought we were made, having a car with glass windows in the doors. To understand that, try and picture coming home at 2 o'clock in the morning from a dance at Cave in the middle of winter, in a car with side curtains with open holes in them.

In fact, I don't think the driver's seat had any curtain at all, so it was very draughty. Most farmers were upgrading their cars, giving up the touring models with side curtains and buying cars with glass to keep out the cold. Farmers were gaining confidence that market prices would keep improving and were spending more money on living expenses.

Another surprise was Mum making a trip south to Dunedin and on to Milton to Harry Wisely's wedding. She stayed in Dunedin with her sister Bessie and seemed to have a good time visiting relations. It was one of the few times that I could remember her taking time out for herself; she even came home with her hair waved.

The last few pages I have written are based on what was written in Mums diaries. As the diaries from 1937 on have been lost, I will write from what I remember, up to 1945, when I started keeping a diary. It gives me a good feeling reading those day-to-day accounts of family life. I feel quite proud and can say, "Yes we made it". Our family came through the tragedy of Dad's death and a terrible depression. We kept on the land that Dad bought at boom prices, while many of our neighbours fell by the wayside.

Mortgage Relief

Many that were still on their farms were kept there through the Mortgage Relief Act passed by the Labour Government. This act was administered by committees, which had the power to wipe off the debt of unpaid interest and rent, and to reduce the amount of capital held on the mortgage. But for that Act, many farmers faced an impossible situation. There were cases of mortgages being reduced by two thirds.

When I suggested to Mum that she should put in for it, she didn't even discuss it, but said, "What we have contracted to do we will do". Mum was a very honest person and I was amazed how quickly she paid the mortgages off and had a clear farm. As I look back years later, many of those who had big debts wiped off did not prosper as families. Other factors in their lives seemed to knock them back.

Mum, who was determined to honestly pay her debts, had a family who in many ways appeared to be better off. The other side of this wiping off of debts was that many elderly people, who had lent money to farmers, were left almost destitute, as their life savings were lost. Maybe there are principles that we need to live by if we expect to prosper.

Mum was really good at finances. She always made good decisions and always seemed to have money when we needed it.

After Dad died, the RSA organized a small pension for each of us children. Once we were back on our feet, Mum wrote to the RSA and said that we did not need the money and more.

Farming Skills

The Saunders

I have perhaps moved ahead a little fast, so I would like to backtrack to 1934 when Mr Gainsford sold his farm and Mr and Mrs Saunders took over, as this brought changes in our lives as well.

The Saunders came from a farm at Mayfield where they had worked for a cousin named Greenslade and it was Mr Greenslade who had bought the farm, putting it in Saunders name to hide some underhand money deal. I didn't discover this until I purchased the farm about ten years later. Len Saunders had grown up in Ashburton and was not from farming stock. They were very hard-working people, but often their management wasn't right, as it was a big change farming on the Cannington hills, compared with the stony flats of Mayfield.

Len had very little understanding of driving a team of horses on hills and was often in trouble with over-worked horses. Of course, I thought I was pretty experienced by this time, so I was able to give him advice in this area. We developed a strong friendship and worked a lot together in many of the annual farm jobs, such as shearing, harvesting and haymaking etc. Being town-bred, he didn't like slaughtering animals for meat, so he bought a lot of their meat from us.

There were two-way benefits. While I was able to help him in the area of stock handling, horse breaking and shepherding, he allowed us to use his woolshed to shear our sheep, and it was in his shed that I learnt to shear. There were no shearing schools in those days, and very few farmers could be bothered taking on a learner, so it was a real benefit to me to have the opportunity to crutch and shear sheep for him.

There was no payment, of course, but at least I was learning to be a shearer. Sometimes this would be done on a wet day, so no time was being wasted.

He also allowed us to travel up the flat on his farm giving us a short cut to the back paddocks of Greenridge. He would also lend us his wagon for carting chaff, enabling us to take a load of fifty sacks compared to twenty-five on a dray.

Boy

Probably the best dog I owned came from Len's carelessness and generosity. He was no hand with a dog, but he had a huntaway bitch, who was very clever. She would bring the milking cows home on her own, leaving the heifers behind. She would have pups almost every time she came in season, and he often failed to get around to destroying surplus pups. As she was seldom shut up, she would get in pup to a variety of neighbour's dogs, so he would never know their pedigree.

Alister & Boy

Tess, the bitch, got cunning and when the pups were growing big enough to be weaned, she would take them out on to the riverbed and hide them so that they couldn't be taken from her. At that time Alister, after he came home from school, would go down the river with old Rover and bring the ducks home. He would shut them in a pen so that they would lay their eggs early in the morning before they were let out for the day. Otherwise, they would be lost, as the ducks would lay their eggs anywhere they happened to be. Duck eggs were a good source of eggs for baking.

One night, he came home with a beautiful yellow-haired puppy, and after consulting Mr Saunders, who declared that he didn't want it, the pup became our possession. We named him Boy. He grew into a lovely long-haired dog. He was very intelligent and could be taught anything a dog was capable of.

Boy was probably a better dog than I could handle with my limited experience, but he became the foundation dog of the team I was to have for many years to follow. I believe that Mr Crawford's dog was his sire.

Boy was a real handy dog who could head, hunt and lead a mob of sheep on the road. He was very noisy for hill work and absolutely silent in the lambing paddock.

From that time on, dogs were to play a large part in both Alister's and my lives. About two years later, Alister got another pup from that same source, and he and I were to have many competitions with one another as we trained our young dogs. We were both to discover that good well-trained dogs were a tremendous aid in sheep farming and driving stock on the road, as motor transport was yet some years away.

Even though there were professional drovers, much of the work of shifting stock on the road was done by farmers and their sons. Horses and dogs were still very important tools for handling stock on sheep and cattle farms, and without their help, there is no way the hills would have been mustered and stock been delivered to the saleyards and meat works.

One of the first jobs we boys did was to drive fat lambs down to the lower Pareora gorge to meet other farmers and a drover, where a big mob of sheep would gather to begin the two-day journey to the Pareora Works. I guess those little jobs were all part of our education to play our part in the farming industry.

Things were changing, and more and more cars were using the roads. Many farmers were giving up their working horses and going over to tractors as they searched for new ways to make up for the lack of progress over the depression years.

Breaking Horses

Dad had been good with horses and had always bred and broken horses. He broke them in the old way, by pulling the horse up to a post and tying it to it. The horse would pull back and fight until it was exhausted and beaten. However, it would often be hard to catch.

Bill Rhodes was a drover who had worked on some of the big stations, like Molesworth. He taught me a new way to break horses. His method was to teach them to lead before he tied them up. He would do this by getting in a small yard with the horse on a rope. When the horse turned to walk away, as it naturally would, he would give it a light flick on the hindquarters with a whip. The horse would then turn back towards him. He would pull it back towards him while talking to it. Every time the horse walked away, he would do the same. The flick with the whip would be quite gentle, but enough to turn it around. Soon the horse would want to stand with its head close to him.

I did not see him break a saddle horse, as he was breaking working horses. To get the horse used to harness, he would hang all sorts of things over its shoulders. Then he would put it between two other horses and drive them around the paddock pulling an old log.

I adopted his methods as they were much easier on the horse than the old way. Once when Alister needed a horse, we rode up to Wilson's at White Rock and rounded up some wild horses that were there. The horse he chose had never been touched before. I got him into the yard and taught him to lead in about an hour. We were able to lead it home.

I loved working with horses and got to be good with them. I grew up in the real horse age, when every farmer had a good horse. All men liked to have a good horse.

Working Horses

When working the team, I would get up at 5 am to feed the horses that would be at the gate waiting. A draught horse takes about 1½ hours to eat a four-gallon tin of chaff. While they were feeding, I would have my breakfast. I would also groom the horses. They sweated a lot and gathered dust, so they had to be groomed every day. After they fed, they would be harnessed up and taken out for a drink.

Rod and Alister Mowing

I would aim to be at work by 7.30 a.m. It would often take half an hour to get to where I was working. We would work till midday, when I would then feed the horses for 1½ hours again. Unless I was close to home, I would feed the horses where we were working. I would tie two half sacks of chaff together and sling them over one of the horses to carry the oats out to the paddock. I would feed the horses with nosebags. They would drink from one of the dams or a creek. In the afternoon, I would work till 5.30 p.m.

When I got home, I would feed the horses again. After tea, I would go out and cover them and give them their second feed. I could not cover them when I first got home, as they would be too sweaty. Later I got the bigger wooden troughs, so they could feed quicker. A six-horse team would eat 3 bags of chaff a day. We grew Garton

Oats, which produced good chaff. Some people fed oatmeal as well, but we never needed to. We grew all our own oats and a contractor would come around each year with a chaff cutter to make the chaff.

Harness

Collars were quite expensive. They had to be relined every few years by the saddlers, who were skilled in repairing them. Each horse had its own collar. You could buy them in different sizes, and they had to fit well. Collars were measured in inches from top to bottom. A horse was always sold with its collar, as it worked into the shape of the horse's shoulders. The chains were attached to the collar. The hanes were a strip of steel going from top to bottom on each side of the collar. The chains were attached to a hook on the middle of the hanes.

I found that horses needed to be well fed. Thin horses were slow and got sore shoulders. Len Saunders' horses had some shocking sore shoulders. I watched carefully, and if one got sore, I would clean it with salty water to harden it up. If necessary, I would cut a bit out of the collar. Sometimes I would rest the horse for a day. A horse would live for twenty years. By the time they were fifteen, they would be slowing down a bit. Old horses were kept on the farm to be used as spares when needed. They could fill in for a day if another horse needed a rest. Our horses were always healthy, because they drank clean water from the river.

When horses were very old, Mr McPherson would take them. I remember thinking that he was very kind to take them off our hands. I later realised that he had a team of rabbiting dogs and needed them for dog tucker.

Each horse had to be treated differently. Our best horses were Bell and Nobby. Bell was a good mare. She had been bred from a hack mare, so she was a good walker. She was a willing puller and worked hard, but she tended to get lean and needed to be well fed. Nobby was a lazy mare, but she was easy to feed and was always in good condition.

Dad had bred these two mares. Each year a stallion would come into the district to mate with the mares. Each man had one stallion that he would take round once a week. Some people liked their horses to be big and heavy like English draft horses. "Purchaser" was the biggest breed. Most New Zealanders preferred Clydesdales, as they were lighter and free moving.

Gordie was a great shafter. He was docile, but very strong. He could turn a dray or push it backwards all on his own. Nothing ever phased him. His only problem was that he was very lazy, so everyone hated driving him. He hated traction engines. When we heard one coming, we would take him somewhere safe. It was only after we sold him at Mr Priest's sale that I realised how hard he would be hard to replace.

Good horses got quite expensive. Mr Gainsford sold the best of his for £60. This was a lot of money when he only got £13 10s an acre for the land. He had looked after them, well and they were fit and strong.

Crop Rotation

We would plough a paddock early in the winter so frost would break down the soil. In the spring after lambing, we would disk it. The paddock would then be sown in turnips or swedes by Christmas. Sheep did not eat hay in those days, even in snow. They all were wintered on turnips. Turnips grew really well, (I remember some as big as footballs), as there were very few weeds in those days.

After the winter the paddock would be sown in oats for chaff for the horses. After the oats, we would take a crop of wheat and then sow back into pasture.

Ploughing

We could plough three acres per day with a six-horse team pulling a two-furrow plough. We used a block and chain system that had been developed in New Zealand to ensure the horses all carried the same load. There would be a big swingle-tree with a two-horse and one-horse swingle-tree attached to it. This would allow

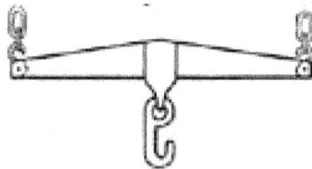

horses to pull three-wide. Another three horses went in front. On each side, a chain went from the collar of the front horse to the pulley on the swingle-tree and back to the collar of the rear horse. This ensured they pulled the same load.

Some people thought the horse with the longest chain had to pull harder, and that the horse on the single-swingle-tree had the hardest load, but I was never sure. Making swingle-trees was big business for blacksmiths. They would make and repair all sized swingle-trees.

The good horses would always be put on the front. The one on the right would walk in the furrow. On a hill, it would have to go up above the furrow. I would call out "Come up out of there!" and it would come up out of the furrow and walk beside it. A good horse could follow a drill or grubber wheel mark or the line of the disks, so you did not need to steer the horses. You just had to make sure that they went right up to the fences before turning around and going back.

The horses were working every day, so they got quite placid. A new horse would be put in the middle at the back. That way, it could

Rod

not cause trouble. Later we used eight horses to pull a three-furrow ride-on plough. There would be four in front with four behind.

For some jobs, we would use five in a row. People said five in a row could pull as much as "six in the blocks". I am not sure if this was true. We used this method for harrowing and grubbing, as the width of the team did not matter. With a plough, the team of horses could not be spread out, as they would not be able to pull while walking on the furrows.

Reaping

A reaper and binder was pulled by three horses. The crossbar on the end of the pole from the binder was attached to the collars of two horses pulling on each side of it. They would pull chains attached to a swingle-tree. The third horse would pull on the side away from the crop. There was no room for a fourth horse between the crop and the horses. Pulling a binder was really hard work as it was very heavy when loaded with grain. The big wheel also powered the binder. The normal practice was to change the horses after three hours.

The first day of the harvest was the hardest, as the horses would have been out of work and would be collar proud. After sowing the turnips at the end of December, Dad would usually turn the horses out in the riverbed. They would be brought in again for the harvest in February and they would be unfit.

I remember one year when Dad had a great crop of wheat up in front of Campbell's, he could not get the horses to pull the binder. He sent me over to Uncle Bob's to get a couple of extra horses. Uncle Bob would always skim a paddock in the summer, so that his horses would be fit for harvest. He gave me two horses to take over. He said that one would "pull like a tiger". I was puzzled because I could not imagine a tiger pulling well.

When I was quite young, Dad had a crop of wheat in the back paddock at Greenridge. The binder had to go straight up the hill, and it was quite steep. Dad got me to sit on the middle horse. He gave me a few stalks of wheat tied in a knot and told me to whack the horses every time they slowed. I was not very keen on the idea, as I was a bit nervous of the binder behind us. However, the horses

91

pulled straight up the hill without a problem, as I made sure they did not stop.

A good farmer would cut an area inside the gate with a scythe the day before starting. This would give a clear area for getting started. After arriving at the paddock, the travelling wheels were taken off the binder. The pole would be taken out from under the cutter and attached to the middle of the binder. With well-trained horses, this could be done without unhitching the horses.

The first round was the hardest, as the horses did not like walking through the crop. The other problem was that you had to take a full cut. On subsequent rounds, you could take a half or three-quarter cut, when the going was tough.

If the binder stopped, you had problems. The cutters would need clearing before you started again. Going up a hill, you let the binder roll back, before starting again. If you stopped in a hollow, it was hard to get started. You would have to tramp the crop, in front of the cutter before attempting to start again.

The binder was an amazing piece of machinery. The cutter could be raised up and lowered down using a lever by the driver. The height could be changed to match the height of the crop. The crop would fall onto the platform as it was cut. It would go up the elevator on to the table, where it was tied into a sheaf. The canvasses often needed repairs. Crops with thick stalks like wheat were quite hard on the canvasses.

An arm would flick the sheaf off so that it would not be in the way on the next round. The alternative was to let the sheaves pile up on the carrier at the back. They could be dropped off five or six at a time, by working some pedals with your feet. On a hill, it was easier to let the sheaves fall off one at a time, but on the flat, we would use the carrier.

The knotters were quite temperamental. You did not touch them if they were going well. Massy Harris had an expert who would come around and check all the binders before the harvest began. If it cut the string too soon or too late, the knot would come undone. Often you could fix the problem yourself, but a lot of time could be wasted, tying up sheaves, if the knotters were not working properly.

Most farms had a reaper and binder. Ours was a Massey Harris. They were the most popular in Cannington, but some people did have McCormick Deerings. They were lighter but could not handle so much crop. The cutter on a binder was 6-feet wide. Some of the later ones were 8 feet wide and were pulled by 4 horses. Mr Gainsford had an 8-foot binder. Campbell's grew a lot of crop, so they had two binders.

The first year after Dad died, Eddie Kelynack did the reaping. The next year Bill Giles drove the reaper. The following year, I did not see why I should be stooking, while Bill sat on the binder, so I took over. I was better with the horses than him anyway. So, I was operating a binder, by the time I was about fifteen.

You could not start reaping until 10 am when the crop was dry. Another man would start stooking at the same time. It was really important to get started, as if sheaves got wet lying flat, they would be really hard to dry. About ten acres could be reaped in a day, before the horses got tired. When the binding stopped at the end of the day, the two men would stook together. I enjoyed working in the evening, because it was cooler.

Two men could stook as fast as a reaper could reap. When not using the carrier, the stooker would do five rows at a time. He would pick up two sheaves from the centre row and put them together. He would bring in two lots of two from the rows on either side.

The stook would have five pairs of sheaves in a row, leaning in towards each other. The grain would be at the top so it would dry. With two men, you could stook 6 rows at a time and could usually stook about 15 acres a day.

Dad usually grew 20 acres of wheat each year. He also had to grow 30 acres of oats to feed the horses. It took a thousand bags of chaff to feed a team of horses for a year. A working horse would eat a kerosene tin and a half of oats in the morning and another tin for lunch and two tins at night. A horse took an hour to eat a tin of oats, as they took a lot of chewing.

Stacking

The sheaves would be left in the stooks for about two weeks before being put into a stack. The sheaves could be put into a stack when they were not fit, but it was best to get them dry.

Harvesting needed five men and two drays. Usually, two farmers would work together. Each farmer would employ a man for the summer. That made four men. We would send a note in to Mr Thoreau in Timaru and the extra man we needed would arrive out on the train the next day.

Most farmers could stack, but only a few were really good at it. Mr Gainsford did our stacking, and he was good. I did a bit of stacking later on, but I did not have enough experience. In Cannington, the stack had to be strong enough to withstand strong winds. A good stack would keep the crop absolutely dry. If it was staying in the stack a while, we would rake the top so that all the straw was like thatch to the outside.

One man would work on each dray and the third in the paddock. He would fork onto the dray. The drivers would stack the sheaves down the side first and then across the back. The corners would be woven together. While one dray was in the paddock being

Binder

stacked, the other would be at the stack being unloaded.

Two men would work on the stack. The "crow" would feed the sheaves to the stacker. This job was often done by a boy or girl. The man unloading the dray could not always see where the stacker was working, but would just fork the sheaves up on the top of the stack. The crow would take the sheaf and put the knot up and ready for the stacker to place. The stacker would place it with the knot down. We got really skilled at forking sheaves.

The stacks would usually be in the same paddock as the crop. A team of five men could complete two stacks in a day. The crop would be left in the stack for six weeks to sweat until it was dry.

The Threshing Mill

Each farmer would have to wait their turn for the mill. The Winter brothers at Albury had two mills that they worked around Cannington. Their father had owned Whiterock. We used Ernie Tozer, who also had two mills.

About ten men would work on each mill. Men were really keen to work on the mills. When they finished a season, they would book in for the next year. It was a tough life. They would start at 6 am in the morning and work until dark, for six days a week, with only Sunday off. Most of the men would be married, and they would stay with the mill for the entire season. If the mill owner was around on Saturday afternoon, he might take a few of the men home to Timaru for Sunday. The mill would keep on working until the early winter, when the men would then go off to other work.

The men lived in small huts called a "stinky", which were really a small wagon with a canvas roof. The cookhouse was a bigger hut, with room for a stove and two beds. The "tanky" and the cook slept in the cookhouse. They would try to park beside a river on Sundays, so the men could have a wash and clean their clothes and catch a fish.

The owner would tell the farmer when the mill was coming. He would bring in the coal in the days before. You would see the smoke of the traction engine coming. The arrival of the mill was quite an event for the children.

Getting up a steep hill could be quite difficult. The engine would go up first, and stop. The men would lay out the cable and winch the mill up. Two men would walk behind the mill with blocks to put under the wheels, if something went wrong. Sometimes they would need a couple of takes to get it up. The mill owner would start charging ten minutes after the mill went in the gate. The men only got paid while the mill was working. They got grumpy, if it was too hard to get into the paddock.

The tanky carted water for the engine using a big tank on a dray. In the early days, they would fill the tank with a bucket. Later on, they had a hand pump and would put a hose in the water and start pumping. If the water had to be carted a long way, it would be really hard to keep up with the traction engine.

One horse would come with the mill, and they would borrow another from the farmer. The tanky would often help the engine driver and they often went on to become drivers.

The mills never seemed to break down. The Clayton mill was popular. They would have been imported from England. Later the tin mills came; they were lighter, but did not do such a good job. In the very early days, the steam engines were stationary and had to be pulled by a big team of horses. I only remember traction engines being used.

A mill could thresh a stack in about two or three hours. We would normally put two stacks side by side, and they would put the mill in between. This enabled them to complete two stacks before moving it. They were well organised and could move the mill quite quickly.

The "feeder" was in charge of the mill. He had a big knife and would pick a sheaf up with the back of the knife. When he turned the knife over, it would cut the string. He had to ensure an even flow into the mill.

Three men worked at the back of the mill. One would be stacking the sacks, and the other two would be sowing by hand. The tanky's first job was to pull some straw around with his horse and lay it out behind the mill. The bags of grain would then be stacked on the straw.

A mill would do our four or five stacks in less than a day. They would then move to another farm. The mill team did everything. The farmer just had to stack the straw. He would often use the straw to winter his cows. Sometimes we would direct the straw elevator over a fence, so we could stack the straw in the next paddock.

We would always try and sell the wheat straight away. The Annands agent would take a sample around the flour mills and try to get a good price. The flour mills did not like wheat with a lot of broken grain. It was a big problem if you could not sell the wheat straight away. The rats and mice would get into the bags and make an awful mess. The birds soon learnt to peck a hole and let the grain run out.

When sold, the grain would be carted to the railway at Cave by truck. In the early days, this was done by horse and dray. I remember the first header that came into the Cannington district. It was down on Mr Cooper's farm. All the farmers came to watch and were very sceptical about it. It was pulled by a tractor.

Young Farmers Club

In 1938 a great boost was given to the Cannington district when a Young Farmers Club was established locally. This was to become an educational tool for up-and-coming farmers. For me personally, this was to bring about a great change in my life. I was a very shy boy with a very limited education and to find myself made the secretary of this new club venture was a real challenge. But it was good for me, as I had to learn to keep minutes, and write letters.

Most important of all, I learnt to stand up and speak to the meeting, something I doubt I would have done, had I not held that office. I believe that I had a real desire to be able to do those things, but fear and shyness would have prevented me daring to attempt them, had I not more or less been forced into that role.

The main role of the club was educational, teaching modern and better ways of farming. Training was done by lectures from Department of Agriculture staff and successful farmers, plus field days and competitions. There was also a social side to the clubs activities, bringing young farmers together for fellowship.

Debating and speech making was also an important part of club activities. This was something that I really enjoyed, and I like to think I became quite good, and it was a skill that was very useful in later years.

Alister too, became quite skilled in this area and became a member of the club's successful debating teams. I am sure that our time in the YFC was an extension of our primary education and played a large part in equipping us to be capable farmers and useful citizens.

Shearing

It was about this time that I took up shearing for other farmers to earn money for the farm that I believed I would someday buy. This had been my private dream since I was quite young. Every penny I earned went into my bank account and I never ever drew any out. I recognised that with three boys in the family, we couldn't all have the family farm, so my plan was to get out and earn one. Shearing was a good way to earn extra money, and good shearers were always in demand. I teamed up with a neighbour's son, Jim Campbell, and we shore together for about twelve years, building up a shearing run handy to home.

With Alan and Alister at home, it was quite easy for me to get away and still be home at busy times on the farm. The shearing sheds in those days were pretty crude compared with modern sheds. The handpieces we called "hot boxes", as they got so hot that they would burn one's hand. They had the same effect on the sheep, making them struggle and difficult to hold. For this reason, we bought our own handpieces, taking them with us from shed to shed. These handpieces were a new improved model and cost us £6 ($12) and served us for many years. This seems to be a very small price compared with today's prices, but we were only receiving 18/- to £1 per hundred sheep shorn. We were not making a fortune quickly, but it was good money at the time.

Because shearers were in short supply, we were soon shearing in most of the sheds in the Cannington district. We were made very welcome and treated very well.

No research had been put into finding a faster technique, so shearing tallies were quite low compared with today. Our tallies

98

were about 150 a day and a shearer who could shear 200 a day was looked upon as something to be seen. We started work at 5.30 am and finished at 5.30 in the evening, but I enjoyed the work as it entailed working for different people as we shifted from shed to shed.

The best sheds were Cannington and Nimrod. Cannington station, where Grandad McKenzie had shorn in the early days, employed four shearers. Nimrod station also employed four shearers. The shearing season was quite short, beginning about mid-October and ending in February.

Lamb shearing was only beginning to take on, and pre-lamb shearing was quite unknown. Except for some crutching in the winter, which didn't take much time, it all fitted into four months, leaving plenty of time for other work.

Mustering

While crutching lambs at Nimrod and Matata with our neighbour Jim Calder, I was introduced to hill country mustering, an occupation I was very keen to take up. As Jim was giving up mustering because he was fully involved on his farm, the Howell brothers invited me to take his place. I jumped at the chance.

On my first day out on the tussock hills, I was a very green recruit having had no experience, and having never even seen a huntaway dog working. I had my handy dog Boy and Alister lent me his Tip to make up my mustering team. I took my place with some fear and trembling, watching carefully what the other men did. I must have done reasonably well as there was no criticism and I seemed to be accepted as if I knew what I was meant to be doing.

They were great men to work with: Wilfred and Ben Howell and Phil Green. Phil who owned a neighbouring grazing run had been a full-time musterer in the Canterbury high country and was a member of the "Flying Gang" well known in the Mid Canterbury area. In his young days, Phil held a record in North Canterbury for being the fastest walker. I would walk up the razorback with him. I would struggle to keep up, but I would not let on to him.

Phil was a man with great dogs, and I learned a lot from him, as to the ways of handling sheep on the tussock hills and bush-filled gullies, and soon built up a good team of dogs for myself. This was the answer to one of my secret boyhood dreams: to be a high-country musterer. I thought in my immature years that this would be the height of adventure. While mustering on the local grazing runs was not quite high country, it satisfied that desire in the meantime.

I loved those days out on the hills with my dogs. Even though it was long days and hard work, there was a feeling of freedom and satisfaction. At Nimrod, we would have a big breakfast at 3.30 a.m. and would be on our way climbing the steep bush-clad razorback ridge, while it was still dark. The aim was to be on the block to be mustered by daylight just as the sheep just moved off their night camps for their morning feed. It was important to have the sheep home and into the holding paddock before the heat of the day. Musterer's pay was between £1 and 22/6 a day.

Nimrod had to be mustered on successive days. The fences had been so ruined by fire and snow that the sheep would drift back through the fences, if they were not mustered quickly. The Howells used fires to burn off the rough grass. They would burn a small block every winter. This way, the fire would never get out of control. If they did not burn an area, it would become impenetrable with snowgrass and matagouri.

I once met Mr Nicholson, who had fenced Matata. He came from the Isle of Skye, had been a shepherd at the Cave outstation of the Levels run for several years before taking up this lease. A bachelor, he built a small hut near the present Matata homestead and proceeded to fence his run. He cut posts out of the bush. Initially, he had no pack-horse and carted posts and wire on his own broad shoulders for 1,000 or more feet up the hillside above his home.

Mr Nicholson knew Granny McKenzie well. He said he never saw a fat sheep come off the Hunter Hills. He did okay, because he would lift the fences in the gullies so his sheep could wander onto Cannington. They would come back fat when the Scott's were shearing or weaning. He was a good hand with dogs, and often mustered on Mount Nimrod, and other nearby properties, after moving to Cannington.

Of course, today with the advent of bulldozers, tracks are built all over those hills and one can ride a farm bike or drive a light truck to the top of Nimrod. This has changed the way the work is done. Cattle keep the rough grass under control.

Those days out on the hill felt like a holiday to me and I enjoyed every bit of it. It also led on to my interest in dog trials, which was the only sport I was ever involved in.

Improving Farm fertility

During this time when I was part-time shearing and mustering, Alan and Alister carried on the farm work, as this was always the number one priority. I believe the farm was gradually improving in fertility and stock carrying capacity. One of the hindrances to improving the pastures on "Greenridge" was the infestation of twitch in some paddocks. It was a real problem, as this plant had a tremendous root system that was almost impossible to destroy.

While standing outside the church waiting for the service to begin, I would always hang around with the farmers to see what I could learn by listening to them. One morning I heard some of the older farmers talking about this very problem. Fred Rapley said that a simple way to destroy this problem weed was to plough the paddock and when the furrows started to get green, to plough it again and again. I was to find that after about three ploughings, the weed was dead and the ground was in great order. These paddocks became the best we had. The same method also worked with Californian thistles, which were a curse at this time, especially when growing grain crops.

I guess the biggest boost to production came from the use of lime spread on the paddocks. This came about from research done by the Dept of Agriculture and passed on, in my case, through lectures and field days organised by the YFC. Some small amounts of lime had been sown when sowing crops, but not enough to have any significant effect. So, the realisation that tons to the acre were needed to sweeten the sour clay soils of South Canterbury was a great discovery. After spreading a ton of crushed lime on a pasture, the results were plain for the eye to see in a few month's time. There was a big increase in grass growth, and clover came into the pasture growing vigorously and bringing about better stock health, heavier lambs and more wool.

Alister and Rod

Some of the so-called poorer soil in the foothill areas became high producing and farms that were abandoned in the depression years became high producing sheep and cattle farms. We were to benefit from this, especially on the "Greenridge" hills. It made sheep and cattle farming more productive than growing crop, so we gave up growing grain, except oats for horse feed.

At the start, lime spreading was hard work, being done with an implement similar to a seed drill, pulled by three horses, and with a big box to contain the lime. The crushed limestone was delivered by truck in 1½ hundredweight sacks and dumped in heaps on the ground at the end of the paddock. The bags had to be lifted off the ground and poured out of the bag into the topdresser to be spread over the paddock. To treat 20 acres, one would have to lift about 300 of those heavy bags, so it is no wonder that many of us doing that work ended up with back trouble.

The first lime we used came from Oamaru, and a government subsidy enabled it to be delivered free by rail to the nearest railway station. There was a lot of manhandling of heavy bags to get a coverage of two to three tons to the acre over the farm, but the results changed farm practice in the Cannington district. The method of spreading changed quickly as crushing plants were established in many places, including one at Cave. Small portable plants came into use, as lime deposits were plentiful.

Truck owners soon caught on to the idea that there was a future in spreading lime, so before long there were spreading boxes available to fasten to the back of flat deck trucks. Later big bulk carrying trucks spread the lime with spinners, covering a wide spread. The flat deck truck was hard to work on, as dragging bags of lime along the deck to feed the lime into the bin at the end of the deck, as it travelled along, required good balance, especially on hillsides. It was a great advance having it all done in bulk.

Timaru Water Supply

This was the beginning of a new prosperity on a lot of farms, brought about by a big increase in stock numbers, more wool, heavier lambs, better crops and of course a better income. Another good thing that happened at that time was that Timaru put in a new water supply for the town, bringing a supply of water by pipeline from the Upper Pareora Gorge. The pipeline came down the Cliffs road, giving the residents a piped water supply off the new pipe.

So for the first time, we had an abundance of fresh, clean water, as much as we wanted at a very small charge, plenty of water for the garden and troughs in the paddocks along the road front.

Rabbiting on Braeval

Mum was not able to pay me for the work that I did on the farm. She provided me with food and shelter and paid for any clothes that I needed, but she could not afford to pay me any wages. The first real money I earned was rabbiting with Eddie Kelynack in the winter of 1940.

Old Alex McPherson had employed Jack Ireland at Braeval, who was an expert on rabbit control, and he was going to clean them all up in so many years. Alex got suspicious of what he was doing, as the numbers did not seem to be declining. He went out himself and put out a line of poison and was absolutely astounded at the number of rabbits that died. The rabbiter was not getting rid of the rabbits at all, but was actually building them up, waiting for a year when the price was good, and then he would make a big kill. Alex was so annoyed that he sacked the man.

He got in touch with Eddie Kelynack to see if he would take on the task of clearing the rabbits. Eddie was an expert at rabbiting. Eddie asked Bob Alexander and me to go with him. I had never seen anything like it. You could just give a whistle and the whole hillside would move.

We would go along the hillside with a hand grubber and chip a bit of soil out and drop in a handful of cut up carrots. On the steep hillsides and rocky places, we would mostly just put it out on the sheep tracks. On the top of the hill, we used a little plough pulled by one horse and would put the carrots in the furrow. The smell of the fresh soil would attract the rabbits. We would feed the rabbits three nights and then miss a night and then lay poisoned carrots.

We got some tremendous kills, and some days we could hardly handle the number of rabbits that we had killed. On an average night, we would kill about 600 rabbits. In the morning we would gather them up. We would have to get out early to beat the hawks. The hawks would soon learn that there would be a lot of dead rabbits and would start carrying them off. They would make an awful mess and would ruin the skins.

Our horse would have a packsaddle, and we would load it up with rabbits. We would dump them in a big heap and skin them. Round the back of the run, we just threw the carcasses down the under-runners. Round the front of the farm, where Alex would be likely to find them, we would dig a hole and bury them. The evening would be spent scraping the fat off the skins. We would put them on wires and hang them out to dry.

Eddie was a real expert on rabbits, and he could not bear to see a live rabbit after we had poisoned an area. He was really fussy about keeping the carrots clean and he would put sugar with the strychnine. This made a syrup that would stick to the carrot cubes. The rabbits died very quickly, and the dead rabbits would be found within five or six yards of where they took the poison.

Eddie liked working at night as he was always "dragging the chain". Bob and I did not like being late and liked to start early in the morning. After a while, Bob and I started to work together and left Eddie to work on his own. That allowed us to start early and knock off early at night. We probably spent about six weeks up at Braeval during that winter. We cleaned up the rabbits to a point where they were manageable, and Bill Little took over after that.

We got £10 for a hundred skins, which was a record price. There was a skin sale in Dunedin every month in those days, so we packed them in sacks and sent them there. The whole country was infested with rabbits, so rabbit skins were big business. I think that my share was about £112. That was the first big cheque that I had in my life.

We struck the good price and Jack Ireland missed out. He was just doing what the rabbiters did in those days, and few of the runholders woke up to it. The rabbiters were mostly trapping, and they would let the does go, so they would continue to breed. They would let the numbers build up until the price was good and then get a big kill. The Young brothers rabbited at Belmont on the Brothers for years and years, but they never killed the rabbits out.

Gran at Riverbank

War Again

Preparing for War

In 1938 the threat of war in Europe was looming as Hitler's Germany built up a powerful army of tanks and aeroplanes and made threatening noises against her neighbouring nations. This was to have a far-reaching effect on NZ that, at that time, we could not even imagine. The first talk of NZ being involved in war was when at a YFC meeting we had a visit from an officer in the CYC (Canterbury Yeoman Cavalry) mounted rifles urging young farmers to join and train as territorials, as part of the NZ army.

Along with several other boys, I spent some weekends training in mounted warfare. We spent a week in camp at Cave living in tents and spending the days trekking over the countryside playing at war, never thinking that NZ would soon be involved in the real thing. I was never very interested in learning about war, but I could see the point in being prepared, and I loved the horse side of it. I was assigned the packhorse to carry a machine gun, and I soon had him trained to walk smartly alongside me and not be hanging back behind me.

There was a bit of glamour in being a member of the "Gentlemen of the CYC", but when I saw how some of them behaved away from home, I did wonder about the gentlemen part.

War

While these good things were happening on the farming front, the threat of war in Europe came into being in September 1939 when Germany declared war and Great Britain found herself at war with Germany. In those days, NZ was very much part of the British Empire, and the NZ government quite quickly declared war against Germany. This was to have a big effect on the NZ way of life for the next six years and beyond.

The NZ government called for volunteers to make up an expeditionary force to train and go overseas to help in the struggle to bring peace again in Europe. Many young men flocked to join up, looking for adventure, while fearing that the war would end before they could leave NZ shores. Little did we think that the war would escalate and continue for years with a tremendous loss of young NZ lives.

This was a very unhappy time for many NZ mothers, including our own mother, who had already lived through one terrible war. This was one of the most difficult periods in my life as I tried to come to terms with what my role should be. I had no great desire to go overseas, I was very happy with my lot as a farmer, and I guess I was a bit mean-spirited in not wanting my plans and dreams upset. However, after much heart

Alister on Goldie

searching, I reasoned that if I went to the war, my brothers would not need to go, so after discussing it with Mum, I went to town and volunteered for service. Much to my surprise, I was turned down on medical grounds. I used to worry about my brothers, thinking wrongly that I would be able to handle difficult situations better than they would. I'm not sure why I had that idea because time was to prove me wrong.

Not long after that Alister was called up as an eighteen-year-old to train as a territorial and spent over a year in training and Alan was conscripted into the army for training to join the NZ Expeditionary forces overseas.

Alan

I would like to record something of Alan, as I knew him, as he is not able to speak for himself as the war machine took him away to his death and robbed him of the life he was born to live. I can only write of what I knew of him before he left NZ to go overseas. The letters he wrote home, which I am sure Mum would have kept, were somehow lost in the process of shifting and getting rid of things that are not deemed to be worth keeping.

Alan was always a quiet, shy boy who was always happy with simple things. He didn't excel in any special way at school, but he was always well behaved and diligent in his work. He left school when he finished primary education at Cannington School. Alan always had a love for growing things. He was always collecting tree seeds and growing them in boxes and later planting them in suitable places. He was a very patient good-natured young man, who never complained or grumbled, and seemed to take life as it came.

He was very different to me, as he wasn't mad about horses, dogs and sheep like I was, but he was quite happy to work in those areas when required. Mum always said she would like him in time to have "Riverbank" as she was sure he would do well on a small piece of land growing trees and plants and keeping pigs and bees. He proved himself in those areas as far as time allowed.

At the beginning of the war, the Government made a call for NZ to increase its production of pig meats. This was done through the YFCs, and they offered some sort of financial help to young men willing to buy a young sow and go in for pig breeding.

The aim was to make the country self-supporting in pig meats. An official from the Department of Agriculture came to a YFC meeting challenging members to get involved. Alan put his name down and was eventually allocated a young sow.

I remember well borrowing a trailer from a neighbour and rigging up some sort of a hitch on the back of our Model T and setting off to Milford to take possession of this pig. The trip wasn't without its problems, as one of the tyres on the trailer was punctured, and the tube was ruined before we discovered it. We ended up having to go to a service station and buying a new tube. The end result was good, and we went home with a very nice Black Devon sow ready to breed and start producing the much-needed weaner pigs. She turned out to be a great producer; two big litters a year that grew into the heaviest weaners I had ever seen.

We were able to get some good timber from a house that was being demolished in Timaru and Alan built a pigsty, big enough to accommodate a dozen pigs. He also fenced some small paddocks to keep the pigs in while they were being fattened. He grew all sorts of feed for them and turned out some great pigs, in the short time he had before he was drafted into the army. He really found his niche there and was very proud of the fine pigs he was able to produce. He also bought store pigs to fatten; one year when there were big crops of potatoes and potatoes were very cheap, he bought potatoes to fatten pigs. I think the biggest litter the sow produced was 17 and as she only had 14 teats. Helen had to rear three of them by hand.

Alan also started into honeybees, and for a time we were eating our own home-produced honey. During that time, we had our first outbreak of foot rot in our sheep. A neighbour driving a mob of his ewes to the ewe fair at Holme station had some infected with footrot. He threw one getting too footsore to travel over the fence amongst our sheep on the riverbed and of course, it spread through our sheep.

It fell to Alan's lot to spend a lot of time getting the sheep clean from that contagious, crippling disease. I had never seen footrot before, so this was something new to deal with, and Alan seemed to have the patience to work day after day dealing with this problem. I don't think we were ever completely clear of foot rot again.

Alan also started to make concrete fencing posts, as a shortage of wooden posts was bringing concrete posts into fashion. Unfortunately, he made them out by the river where water and shingle was easily available, but a flood came before they were shifted and many were washed away. Yes, I think Mum was correct. Alan would make a good small landowner, but of course, it wasn't to be.

MISSING.—Private Alan G. McKenzie, son of Mrs. M. McKenzie, "Riverbank." Cave.

Looking back now I think Alan's main strength was his faith in Almighty God, and I believe it was that belief that enabled him to persist at monotonous tasks and to take army life in his stride.

In spite of my fears and doubts, he seemed to enter into army life without any problem. He joined the Medical Corp and made friends with like-minded young men. After he finished his training, he spent some time at home on sick leave, as he was troubled with some kind of chest infection. He spent that time helping neighbours with their harvest, as by this time, farm labour was very scarce. It wasn't long before he was declared medically fit again and was sent overseas to join the military forces in the Middle East in the battle zone. He sent home to Mum very interesting letters on his experiences in the army and other travels when on leave.

He had a trip to Israel, which was of special interest to him, as he was able to visit the sites that he had become familiar with in his study of the Bible. The last Mum heard from him was in Italy where he was posted as missing.

One of his mates had written to Mum telling how he had gone for a walk in a village one evening and had not been seen again. Even though they had made a search for him, no trace of what had happened was found.

At the beginning of 1945, Mum wrote in her diary:

> Our soldiers are still in Italy fighting a long hard struggle in bitter winter. It is over seven months since Alan was missing and we have not received any further word of him, but hope that we might hear that he is a prisoner. It is over two years since he left NZ and we trust this year will see peace again and all our soldiers home again.

We held on to the hope that he would turn up amongst the prisoners of war, which would be released at the end of the war. But that hope did not materialise, as nothing further was heard of him. Looking back now, I am aware of how hard that time must have been for Mum; all the waiting, the fears and eventually heartbreak. Mum had been very fond of Alan.

Looking back, I am conscious of the thoughtlessness of youth, as I don't remember showing any special concern for Mum as she bore the loss of one of her children, knowing that in this life she would never see him again. I guess I was wrapped up in doing my own thing, perhaps being even quietly excited about my own future which had so much to offer.

Mum bore her sadness quietly and bravely, as she had borne other knockbacks in the past. I now know that she had an inner strength that came from her faith in God. It brings tears to my eyes as I write and think back how she might have been even hurt by the callousness of her eldest son. I do remember that I did not go out and celebrate when peace in Europe was declared, as my heart was sad. On 16 August, Mum wrote the following words in her diary.

> Peace celebrations were held everywhere. Helen, Alister and Uncle Jack went to Cave to celebrate. Alister played football. I made Marmalade. No word of Alan. If he had returned, what a happy time it would have been and how different peace would have seemed.

War Effort

The war was to make a big change in our way of life, as it was to most New Zealanders, as everything was geared towards the "war effort", in other words, helping England to survive. The NZ farmer's main role was to make NZ self-supporting and to increase the production of meat and wool for export to Great Britain.

The imports of oil, petrol and steel were cut to a minimum, so there was rationing of many items that we were used to having free access to. We were given coupons for petrol, butter, sugar and even clothes. There were restrictions on travel by train, and a person who resided at Pleasant Point could not get a ticket to travel past Ashburton.

The train and the NZR bus from Fairlie went down the main road to Timaru. The YFC got on the case, and the NZR bus started going down through Mawaro, Cannington and Holmes Station. This made getting to town much easier.

The government took over the total production of meat and wool, so that farmers wouldn't make a fortune out of the war as had happened in the past. Many items such as fencing wire, machinery and parts, and anything made of steel was difficult to come by. Farm workers were in short supply as young men were conscripted into the army and factories making munitions. There were manpower committees set up in every district to see that workers were placed where they were needed. As the war went on and we were threatened with invasion from Japan, all homes and cities were "blacked out". Not a light was to be seen at night – the land was in total darkness.

Home Guard

A "Home Guard" was established throughout NZ where local men were trained in the art of war. Old soldiers from the first world war came out of retirement from the army and were recruited to be officers and trainers to mould the shop-keepers, farmers, and essential workers into a fighting force to defend our nation in the event of an invasion from an enemy nation.

A group was formed in Cannington-Cave, local farmers became officers, and I was made a corporal. This group of very busy farmers met every Saturday afternoon, to be trained and drilled into an army of sorts. To begin with, we had no weapons except some sporting rifles, so we were trained using sticks pretending they were rifles. In time, old 303 rifles that had been used by territorials in the past were introduced. We did get some training with an old machine gun and some hand grenades.

Rod and Alan Lamb at CYC

We spent a night on Caroline Bay digging trenches and getting prepared for any invasion that might eventuate. We were told that these were front line trenches from which there would be no retreat. We were a pretty ragged fighting force, and I think it would be the height of imagination to think that we could stand against a trained invading army. But it did bring home to us the dangerous position that NZ was in. In the early stages of the war in the Pacific, we would have been facing the enemy with old 0.22 sporting rifles. Thank God, it never happened.

During this time, many changes were taking place, but I find it difficult to put them in the order that they occurred, though they are fixed in my memory without any diary recordings. At this time, Alister was away training in mechanised warfare, because by this time horses in war were recognised as out of date. He trained at Stewart's Gully near Christchurch and also at Waiouru in the North Island.

It amazes me how all the farm work got done because farm labour was very scarce with many young, able-bodied men overseas, plus the 18-year-olds who were in camp in NZ. Many women helped on farms, some girls becoming full-time land girls. Many farmers carried on with the help of their wife or daughter. I continued with my shearing and mustering work and fitted the farm work in with this. Of course, there was no maintenance work being done on farms as fencing wire and posts were virtually impossible to procure. But the harvest and the shearing did get done, and the lambs were all tailed, and the cows always milked.

Shearing during the War

With all the young men away at war, getting the sheep shorn was difficult. Older men, who had retired from shearing, made new moccasins, bought new handpieces and went out shearing again. One man in our district, who was over 60 years of age and had not shorn over a hundred sheep for many years, teamed up with an old mate who was a very thin old man and they were shearing 400 sheep between them, seven days a week. I shore with this thin old man who was twice my age, and he could run rings around me. I was amazed at his skill in shearing very tough sheep.

One year at Mt Nimrod, the boss's brother, a first world war veteran, and I did the mustering and the shearing helped by a learner shearer, who was waiting to go into camp. We would have breakfast at 3.30 am in the morning and climb out over the bush-covered razor-back to arrive out on the block to be mustered as it was getting light. We would muster the sheep off and have them yarded by late morning and then spend the rest of the day shearing.

The next day would be spent shearing and getting the sheep out again, and then we would repeat the process over again. There were no bulldozed tracks in those days, so most of the mustering was done on foot. Jim Campbell and I did most of our travelling from shed to shed on horseback or by my horse and gig.

Entertainment

I don't want you to get the idea it was all work and no play because that wasn't the case; there were wet days when outside work could not be done. Also, there were lots of dances and euchre parties; we

115

could handle getting home from a dance at 2 am and being on deck for work the next day.

Because there wasn't much petrol available for travelling to dances, the local carrier, who also ran a school bus, would use the bus to take us to dances. Some romances began in the dark of that bus and marriages were the result. The dances of those days were great fun, as in a country district, residents of all ages joined in.

The dancing was very different from what is known today. The dances were mostly all old-time where a boy and a girl would dance together and would dance with a number of different partners throughout the evening. The girls and some older women would sit around the edge of the hall, school, or woolshed and the boys and men would stand around the door talking and smoking. When a dance was announced, they would stamp out their cigarettes and rush across the room for a partner.

I would make a point of having every dance and for the popular dances, square dance or novelty dances. You had to be quick, or you would miss out, as all the girls would be taken. To be sure of a partner, one could "book" a girl several dances before, so as to get a good dancer for those special dances.

The dance was controlled by an MC (Master of Ceremonies) and for many functions, I played that role. The MC had to announce the dance and be prepared to get up and start the dance off, and for the square dance, he had to call each figure to keep everyone dancing the same figure at the same time.

The band would be made up of the piano and probably a violin and banjo. The cost for a band of that sort would be £1 ($2) for the evening, and they would play from 8 pm to 1.30 am and sometimes to 2 a.m. We thought these dances were great fun and it was there that boys met girls and many life-long romances would begin.

There was never any sleeping in the morning after a dance, as work had to go on as usual as the work ethic was very strong in those days, at least it was in our family. We used to kid ourselves that a late night didn't make any difference to our ability to work the next day. Dances were mostly held on a Friday night, so there was only one day to go and then a Sunday rest.

116

Ellen Cleland

In 1942, Ellen Cleland came and boarded at Riverbank. The teacher who was boarding with us went overseas to the war, and she came as a relieving teacher until an appointment could be made. We had heard that the next teacher would be a woman and I was really against boarding her, because I had not had a happy experience with women teachers at school. I thought that they were all bits of dragons. Helen was determined that she would come and board, and in the end, she and Mum won the day.

Prior to that, I had been praying that God would bring what I called a "church girl" across my path. I really wanted to get married and I could not imagine being married to a girl that didn't go to church. None of the girls that I knew went to church. I prayed that God would bring a church girl across my path and next thing this teacher arrived. I was getting better at praying by then.

I was up at Campbell's helping with harvest on the day she arrived, so I did not see her. By the time I got home late at night, she was already in bed. I was away again early in the morning, before she came out. Each night, Mum and Helen would talk about what a lovely girl the teacher was, so I thought that I had better check this out, so I made an excuse to go home early for my meal and have a look at her. I got a surprise when I saw her, because she did not look like the school teachers that I had known when I was younger.

A short time later, when Helen was away, the Campbell's rang up and offered to take Helen and me to a dance at Cave. Mum was really determined that Ellen should go, because she thought that she would not stay in the district, if she did not get to know people. She and I went to this dance.

It was funny, because Jim Campbell would usually drive the car, but on this occasion, his brother Jack took charge of the car and was driving. We set off up the road with Jim and Jack in the front, and Jean Campbell and Ellen and I were in the back. Going around the school corner, he went too wide and went off the road on the left-hand side, tipping us all in a heap in the back of the car.

When we were coming home, I expected Jack to go down over Martin's crossing and drop us off at Riverbank, but he just drove straight to his own home over the Cliffs Bridge. Petrol was really short at that time, so I said that if he stopped at his place, we would walk home. We got to walk home together, and that was the first time that I got to talk to Ellen alone.

I had a real inferiority complex and thought that if a girl knew about what had happened to Dad, she would not want anything to do with me. I assumed that Ellen did not know, but her Uncle Bob had already told her. I knew early on that she was the one for me.

Helen did not like us being together and tried to keep us apart. On a Sunday, we would be sitting talking on the seat that Uncle Jack built at the front of the house. Helen would be out every few minutes and shake a mat. She was checking to see what we were doing, but I don't know what she thought we could get up to.

Ellen was only there for a short time, before she got a permanent job at Pleasant Point. It turned out to be a better position. I would ride or bike over to Totara Valley each Sunday to see her.

Rod and Ellen with Alan

In the following March, I asked Ellen to get engaged, and she accepted. She was a little surprised because she would have been happy to carry on being friendly for longer. I was excited about her and was worried that someone might come along and head me off. She did not seem to worry about what had happened to my father. I believed that she was an answer to my prayers.

Wisely Family

I would like to record something of Mums brothers and sister who played a part in our family life in the 1920s and 1930s.

Bessie

Bessie was Mum's sister, who never married. She spent most of her working life as a housekeeper for a wealthy solicitor's family in Dunedin. Bessie had had infantile paralysis as a child. She had one leg shorter than the other and wore a big boot with a sole about 4 inches thick.

Bessie seemed to be a very stern no-nonsense person, with strong Presbyterian principles. She was the sort of person who always thought she was right. She was a very argumentative woman, and you could never argue with her and win. She would never give in or admit she was wrong.

Bessie always came and stayed two weeks at Christmas time. In spite of her annoying habit, she was very good to us as children. She was a very generous lady and always gave each of our family a £1 note ($2) for a Christmas present and again for our birthdays, quite a handsome present in those days. I never spent mine, but put it in the Post Office Savings Bank to keep for the deposit on the farm that I dreamed I would buy.

If Mum's brother Alex came when she was staying, they would spend most of the time arguing. Margaret tells of the time that she was travelling with Aunt Bessie on the train to Dunedin and she argued most of the way as to how to pronounce a word.

The first wireless set our family had was a gift from Bessie. When she could no longer use her old bicycle, she gave it to us. We all learnt to ride it and just about rode it to death. I think she provided for some of Margaret's costs while she was at Teacher's training college too.

She was very strong and would be straight into work as soon as she arrived. She was a bit of a trial to Mum as I think she thought she should be doing work about the place to help Mum. She was always ripping into something, like a piece of the garden, which Mum didn't really need her to do. She meant well, but I think her energetic way left Mum feeling tired.

Bob Wisely

Bob had always farmed close to us, so our families always spent a lot of time together, visiting one another and picnicking together. Bob also helped us with work and advice after Dad's death. At harvest time, he would send his men over with a dray and team of horses to help us. I think Bob was a great comfort to Mum at that time. Mum and Auntie Eleanor talked to each other on the phone, every day except Sunday, when we always met at church.

Wiselys, McKenzies and Tooleys

Bob's farm was quite small (220 acres), but he farmed it very intensely growing good crops. This must have paid well, as he always seemed well-off financially. I remember him as a very nervous careful man who always played things safe.

Alexander Wisely came to Dunedin from Drumblade, Aberdeenshire Scotland on the Grasmere in 1862. Helen Adam had come on board the Philip Laing in 1848, but she was still a babe in arms (daughter of James Adam). Later these two married.

Adam was one of the first four Dunedin City Councillors. He was a shipwright by trade, went farming, came to Dunedin, and made several official trips back to England to help select suitable immigrants for New Zealand.

> When Mr Wisely and Helen Adam married, they went farming in Milton, where Robert Wisely was born. Amongst other toils, his mother used to go out building sod walls, and sowing gorse on them for fences, and all for ten shillings (ie one dollar) per chain. When he grew up, Robert married Eleanor Tooley. In 1913, Robert Wisely bought Pine Terrace from James Lowe. It still required developing, and this was the task that he faced, and which over a period of years, he set out to do. First of all many of the original fences required to be renewed or made good. In order to make smaller fields, new fences had to be erected. This improved the efficiency of the whole farm.
>
> Some fields required draining and this was attended to. Many of the pastures were old and run out, so it was necessary to cultivate the ground for root crops and resow it with modern grasses and clovers. Wheat was always a payable crop, and over the years, a considerable area would be harvested. Finally, many of the sheep were still fine-woolled. Some were almost pure Merinos and many still halfbreds and three-quarter breds.
>
> Gradually he introduced the long-woolled varieties of Romneys and Leicesters, which were both wool producers and meat producers. Refrigeration made it much more payable to discard the Merinos and develop the two-way breds (Allister Evans – The Silver Tussock).

Alex Wisely

Alex was the next to come into the picture when he and daughter Margaret came to live in Timaru in the 1920s. Their house was on the corner of Wai-iti Road and Seddon Street. Alex had farmed in the Milton district, probably near Milburn, where he married a local girl. They had one child, a daughter Margaret. When Margaret was quite young, her mother developed TB. There was no cure for TB in those early days, so it eventually brought about her death at a young age. Alex nursed her himself, during the time she was laid low in bed. He was left with a daughter to bring up, and a fear that she too might contact the dreaded TB.

The reason they came to Timaru was to be in a warmer climate, where he reasoned there would be less risk of Margaret developing TB. Little did he realise that he was the one who was carrying the disease. Not many years later, after a trip to England by boat, he took ill, while crossing the equator, where the heat of the climate was too much for him. Upon arriving home, he was diagnosed as having TB, and he never recovered. The disease that he feared so much and from which he spent so much trying to protect Margaret was to bring about his own death at an early age. Margaret never got TB and went on to live to a big age.

Margaret and Alex spent a lot of time travelling to places where Alex thought the climate would be healthy. TB patients were sent to Waipiata where there was a special hospital. As a precautionary measure, Alex and Margaret spent time holidaying in the South Island high country, Tekapo and Ranfurly being favourite places.

Alex and Margaret visited us a lot at Riverbank, so the two Margarets became good mates. To distinguish between them, we named Margaret Wisely, Cousin Margaret. During the fruit season, Uncle Alex would go to the auction rooms in town and purchase apricots and peaches for Mum and Helen to preserve in jars, for out of season use.

This was a blessing for our family, as bottled fruit made up a big part of our pudding diet in the warmer months of the year. Uncle had the time to spend at the auction looking for bargains. They would come out on Saturday with a carload of fruit and spend the day with us.

Uncle Alex's wife had inherited money. He also made a lot of money out of growing wheat during the Great War. He sold his farm and retired quite young. During the depression, when he was threatened with Mortgage Relief, he just said he would go down and take the farm back. The issue of Mortgage Relief was never raised again. He was careful with money.

Uncle Alex would bring his gramophone and a box of records and we would have an evening of gramophone music, a common practice in those days. I guess this worked two ways as Uncle Alex and Margaret probably enjoyed coming out into the country to a meal prepared for them. We were the only family they had any contact with. They were

Bessie, Jack, Margaret & Alex Wisely

probably both lonely for friends as Alex seemed to keep Margaret on a very short leash and she had very few girl friends of her own age. Alex was the same, as he didn't seem to have many male friends. We were probably good for them, and they were certainly good for us. Cousin Margaret eventually got married and moved to Northland.

Jack Wisely

The other member of Mum's family, whom we came to know really well, was her brother Jack. Jack started on a farming career in the Milton district, working for his Father on a property called "Bankhead". When we were in Milton recently, I made inquiries as to its whereabouts, but wasn't able to find anything about it. I know it was flatland that was wet and needed draining. Jack used to talk about the miles of tile drains they had put in and the many miles of mole drains. He had photos of two traction engines pulling a big mole plough on the property.

Jack came to Canterbury with Bob and they bought a farm at Winchester near Temuka. Like most young men, they met girlfriends and married, causing them to dissolve the partnership. Bob shifted to Cannington where he spent the rest of his life. Prior to the Winchester venture, they had toured NZ and some of Australia on bicycles, so they were really quite adventurous for the times. It was no mean feat travelling the NZ roads on the type of bike available in those days. There were no gears on the bikes being manufactured around the turn of the century.

I think they worked on farms as they journeyed around. I know they spent some time working on "Longbeach", a big station in the mid-Canterbury District. Knowing Uncle Bob in later years, I couldn't imagine him embarking on an adventure like that as he always seemed a very cautious man who always played it safe.

Jack married a Temuka girl called Bertie Watson. She was the daughter of a Temuka coachbuilder whose gigs and buggies were well known around South Canterbury.

They farmed for a while at Winchester and then shifted to Southland for a time. Bertie was an artistic girl with a gift for painting, writing and handwork. She and Mum were good mates in their Winchester days. Bertie didn't like living in Southland and pined for Canterbury, so Jack sold the farm in the south and bought a farm in Methven district in Mid Canterbury.

This was in the early 1920s when land was booming and prices very high. His farm was sold up during the depression.

Uncle Jack in Hillview Garden

While they were in Methven, their marriage broke up. Jack was a very determined man, who wanted his own way. I suspect that he would not have put any effort into his marriage. After his farm was sold, Jack went to work for Gordon Scott near Methven. Later he managed a farm for a lady up near the Selwyn River. He was a very hard worker, but he was very difficult to please.

When he had a serious heart turn, he came down to stay with Mum. He saw Dr Birch in Timaru, and he told him to go to bed. Mum and Helen nursed him until he started to improve. He started getting up each day and began to get his strength back. He went to see the Doctor and asked him if he was meant to come back and see him again. The doctor said he did not expect to see him out of bed again.

Jack went home from the doctor determined to get better. The problem with his heart was that it beat too fast. Provided he stayed on his pills, he was fine. He actually outlived many of his family and did not die until he was 85.

He started grubbing gorse to get back his strength. He also got a large Totora log from Jim Calder. He stood it up on its end and sawed it into slabs with a cross-cut saw. This timber was used to make several tables and stools.

Jack was very handy and would turn his hand to most tasks. He was very impatient, so everything had to be done in a hurry. He was also stubborn and determined.

Jack went up to Marlborough and built a house for Mr Isit from Fairlie, with just a boy helping him. He built the Hillview house for Mum, when Alister got married. He also built the haybarn out of larch poles and tar drums at Parira.

Jack was quite social. Everybody liked him. He was fun to have around and we always enjoyed his visits.

Alex and Cis McKenzie

Alex was Dad's brother. He had a dairy farm at Otakaike. He sold it during the land boom. He must have left some of the money in the farm on a mortgage, so he spent the rest of his life trying to get more money out of the man who had bought it. Mortgage Relief wiped off some of the debt.

Alex had made his money rabbitting when young. He shot rabbits with a shotgun. During that time, you could stand and shoot and the other rabbits would not even move. He was happiest when out shooting with his gun and his dog.

When I first remember him, he was renting the schoolhouse at Hazelburn and doing odd jobs. He suffered a lot from depression, and Aunt Cis had to keep him going. Their only daughter had died when she was twenty-one, and he never recovered.

They had fifty acres at Kakahu that Aunt Cis had inherited from her father, Bullocky Jones. Uncle Alex never seemed to work much, as long as I knew him. They were able to live very cheaply and would be getting a bit of interest from time to time.

Neither Uncle Alex gave Mum much help or advice. This surprised me, as they had both been farmers and were still quite young when Dad died.

Uncle Alex and Aunt Cis came back to Nesscroft when Granny died. Uncle Alex was a beneficiary of the will, so he could not buy it. He bought the property in Aunt Cis's name.

Mum was the main beneficiary of Granny's will, as she got double what Dad's two brothers got. Granny was disappointed in Jim and Alex as they had not really supported her. Dad was the one who looked after her. He would buy a few steers for her each spring and sell them in the autumn. He made sure she had a cow to milk. She took Dad's death really hard, and I don't think she ever really got over it.

Hillview

In 1946, Ellen and I got married and moved to live at Parira, which I had purchased from Len Saunders. Alister took over the responsibility for Riverbank, but we continued to work together and share the team.

When Alister and Shirley got engaged, Mum paid for the Hillview house to be built about halfway between Riverbank and Parira. Uncle Jack did all the building work, with a little help from Alister and I for the heavy lifting. The house had two bedrooms.

When Alister and Shirley got married, they moved into Riverbank. Mum moved down to Hillview and lived there until she died. Hillview had a lovely sunroom at the front, so it was a nice home for Mum. She had a good flower garden and grew her own vegetables. The grandchildren from both houses would visit often, and she would always give them a piece of chocolate and a peppermint. The boys would deliver a billy of milk in the morning and drop off the newspaper at night.

Uncle Jack lived there with Mum most of the time. He also built a woodshed and some hen houses across the road. He had a workshop for his tools and continued making furniture for many people. He continued on there after Mum died in November 1958. He kept the flower garden and always grew sweetpeas along the front fence. He picked off every seed-head that formed, so they kept flowering right into autumn. Everyone who drove past really enjoyed the colour.

The Family at Hillview

www.ingramcontent.com/pod-product-compliance
Lightning Source LLC
Chambersburg PA
CBHW060515030426
42337CB00015B/1899